TRANSFER YOUR CONFIDENCE

Unlock Inner Strengths
That Conquer Insecurities

By

Kathleen Solmssen

in - joy
xxx ooo
Kathleen

DEDICATION

I am so pleased to dedicate this book to my husband Peter. 15 years ago, at a party on Independence Day, he observed a few characteristics in me that prompted him to get down on one knee with a ring in his hand the following weekend. He couldn't avoid my outrageous sense of humor and my love of people. In the weeks that followed, he enjoyed my creative spirit in jewelry, writing, design, fashion and charities. Over the years, Peter has encouraged me, supported me and nearly gotten pom poms out to cheer me on in all of my artistic endeavors. Creative people have their highs and lows. Peter has been there to pick me up and applaud me as well. Every evening, he would read the "missive of the day" with no "corrections or additions to the minutes". A chance meeting on July 4th 2001 was nothing short of a miracle for me.

INTRODUCTION

I write a column called *Pizzazz* for JO LEE Magazine, a lovely international publication with millions of readers. A few months ago, I said to my husband "I think I've come up with an interesting concept for my next column: "*Transfer Your Confidence*s". After I explained this idea, he said: "this a terrific idea, but it isn't an article...you have the makings of a book here...GO FOR IT". I am neither a psychology professional, nor an author of self-help books. The idea for "*Transfer Your Confidence*" just evolved out of living and observing life. I dreamed up this idea for myself in order to stay happy and to get out of the down side of life as soon as I find myself unhappy. It's also about empowering aspects of my personality where I have little or no confidence at all. It's literally about transferring your existing confidences (we all have some) into an area of our lives where we lack confidence

Years ago, a friend said: "I'm labeling you: a 'country philosopher' because you don't read books about how to make life work... you discover ideas on your own and then write about your thoughts in such an understandable and unique way." I hope that he was right, and that this new way of addressing issues on which the reader might have given up hope is as helpful as it has been to me.

CHAPTER ONE
Baby Steps

"If we all did the things we ARE capable of doing, we would literally astound ourselves." --Thomas Edison

They are such naturals. We all envy such people (which is a nice way of saying "we are all terribly jealous" because, time and time again, they do "it" with such ease and grace).

"It" refers to an innate talent, a gift since birth, where a certain task is completed to perfection, in nearly record time, *every* time. We are all born with our own unique "it" expertise. Be still for a moment...dig down...you'll soon discover your "it". We all take "it" for granted and figure, everyone does "it" the same way I do "it" without even thinking about "it". This is simply not true.

Constantly reminding ourselves about what we *cannot* do seems to be a "put on the brakes" approach to life. Time and time again our "monkey mind" inevitably leads to negative head chatter. Like a wild stallion, we need to corral our thoughts and remember: we are all in charge of what goes on just behind our eyes and in between our ears.

Imagine a baby taking his first steps. He falls, he gets up, and he falls again and begins again and again and again. "Safe" is such a boring spot to live in. Adrenaline isn't shooting through a safe person's veins...nor is a creative spirit flowing. Success is trying again and again and again. Have a little chat with that person in the mirror saying: "YOU CAN DO THIS" over and over and over again. After one baby step of accomplishment... get back to your mirror and say: "HOORAY FOR ME" over and over and over again. A step out into the unknown is thrilling and oh, so rewarding. You may become an expert... this new "it" will (if you will it) become second nature. Still and all, you may not like what you always wanted. This matters not...back to the mirror: "I DID IT"! Or try something else.

After years of practice, I have learned how to change the "can't do it noise" in my head to *Transferring my Confidence music*" in my brain. As kids, we'd say: "CAN'T never did anything until TRY came along". To avoid being bullied or called a sissy, I'd always TRY on the playground. Skinned knees healed as pride ensued. Sometimes, being a tomboy was the only way to survive. Today, those brave roots serve me well. Being a risk taker, in a safe way, sort of stomps out any and all "fight or flight" energy. Sometimes I wonder: "who is in charge of me anyway?" Back to the baby taking his first steps. Granted, parents' encouragement helps the child. But every baby walks...I've never seen one crawl through life. We all have an "inner couch", supporting us and coaxing us away from failure and quitting. I have a few talents on my confidence list that... in the past had been on my "won't even try/no can do" list. This may feel like a therapy session; truth to tell, writing was never ever an option for me. Report cards are still a nightmare of a memory. Once doctors discovered A.D.D. (Attention Defect Disorder) and put me on a "concentration" drug, I could READ! But the medication made me feel medicated... so that didn't work.

Teachers would forever say to me: "You can't read, write or spell... you'll never make it through college or for that matter, find a job". Slowly, without an option, I "*Transferred my Confidence*" from painting & design to reading and remembering. To this day, you'll never see me sitting in an easy chair, page-turning a book. Before I finish a preface/introduction, my creative juices pull me off the chair and into the kitchen, on to the drawing board or into my jewelry workshop.

OK, so let's all be astounded with ourselves. Here's how: make a list of 5 inherent attributes.   Don't be shy: be proud. Because you've always had them, over the years these qualities might have been taken for granted.   Embrace them. Visualize your list hanging in a lighted golden frame. Be thankful: treasure each one. In a second column, write down your wish list, i.e., five talents you might have tried to attain and failed, or perhaps you haven't ever tried to accomplish...because it isn't anywhere near your comfortable, familiar wheelhouse. Now, take a leap (like jumping out of an airplane).   It's a jump... a deep dive into your "inner" belief in yourself.   Begin by: "BEING 100%" in your five "natural born" attributes. Then, like a curious, fearless daredevil kid..."*Transfer Your Confidence*"... one talent at a time.... from your powerful "natural born" attributes to your "noisy, scary, can't do it" " list. As the Nike swish says: "JUST DO IT"

CHAPTER TWO
Overcoming Fears

"We gain strength, and courage, and confidence by each experience in which we really stop to look fear in the face...we must do that which we think we cannot." – Eleanor Roosevelt

I have a dear friend whose eldest is about to tie the knot. Her daughter, knowing how utterly shy my pal is, went ahead anyway...way beyond her mother's comfort zone...with a simple "insisting emphatically" request, without a trace of empathy, that her mother give a toast at the wedding reception. Knuckle-white and shaking from head to toe, she relayed this "non-negotiable' demand to me. "I'd never want to hurt my daughter, but I cannot do this... I just cannot do it. I adore my daughter and our son-in-law to be and I could write a very touching toast, but getting up in front of a roomful of friends and trying to utter one single word, well... just thinking about it has me in total panic mode".

I really felt her pain and suggested that we take a walk and talk about life and the upcoming nuptials. Of course, our conversation kept circling back to the dreaded toast. In the middle of her fragile and full-of-fear craziness, I changed the subject: "Are you still responsible for all of the accounting at your husband's office and his clinic too?" "Sure am; I become a night owl as I organize all of the clinic's statements & ledgers while stuffing and stamping the office bills. It's like clockwork. The same ole' same ole' every month. To be honest with you, it's my pleasure. Actually, I *love* doing it.   As you can imagine, I'm never ready to hit the gym the next morning, but I feel so satisfied that all of the ducks are back in their proper rows and all of the envelopes are sealed." In total amazement, I said: "WOW that's fantastic!   On any given month, I'd have a better shot at balancing on one foot all day long, than even ever attempting to balance my checkbook".

It was time for one of our weekly "walk-talk" sessions where we trade-off listening and learning from each other.   "So, the numbers game is your forte; clearly it's your comfort zone. You must feel great with the success you have in that arena, right?" "You've got that right; numbers are my 'A' game.   Come to think of it, I'm also quite proud of my organizational skills as well. I could organize your kitchen, your closets, even your garage to perfection."
"OK" I said as we rounded the edge of a lovely stand of cedar trees... "I've got a game for you... want to play?"

"Game on", she replied. We sat down on a couple of freshly cut oak firewood stumps.   I took her hands in mine as I said very softly yet with firm intention: "in this moment, imagine how you feel each month as you put all of that important paperwork and yourself to bed". Smiling, she said: "pretty damn great!" "And how would you feel if you ever organized my closets?" Laughing, she said: "your closets...*all* of them? I'd merit taking home the gold and it would be a blast...let's do this!"   I said: "Hold your horses cowgirl, not so fast...this game isn't quite over...we haven't reached the finish line. So numbers and organizational skills are as easy as falling off this log, right?". She said: "Yes...it's work, disciplined concentration and earned confidence.   Best part: I win every time."

Once more, I took her hands in mine, looked deep into her eyes...to the core of her being, as I asked: "right now, this minute, I want you to 'BE' that person who always wins in the numbers and organizational skills.   Close your eyes and really, really be there.   Are you there?" With wonder and curiosity she replied: "yes, I am there!" Continuing, I said: "All right, now: let the game begin: *Transfer Your Confidence* from your well-honed skills...to walking up to the dais at your daughter's wedding and with all the love and joy you feel in your heart…. share your prepared toast. Trust me, it will be excellent and you will be brimming with pride.   Game over. OK, let's circle up the wagons and head home and find our happy hour". She was a champion on the dais and loved every moment of pride in herself and her daughter.

CHAPTER THREE
I Can Do It

In the seamstress arena, Lily is the most gifted person I have ever met. In one afternoon...one long afternoon, she can produce an exquisite couture-like garment.... without ever looking at a pattern or a simple drawing. Even though I have absolutely no interest in sewing, needless to say, I am in awe of her talent.

Recently, at the end of a day of creating the most gorgeous evening gown imaginable with complex and intricate details, Lily was bursting with energy! She is a true expert in her field and she knows it. "It's just what I do. I have chosen to be the best". Years ago, as luck would have it, we met, sitting on our mats in yoga class. Don't ask me why, but in some of the most difficult poses, I can nearly twist into a pretzel shape while maintaining my yogi empty mind. Maybe because I'm so tall, maybe because my tomboy within is still alive. Lily, on the other hand, is afraid to venture off of her mat. "I can't stand on my hands, I simply can't and I never will." "Lily, how can you expect your body to invert into a handstand when you keep saying I CAN'T???"

After our class, we relaxed on our mats while talking about that gorgeous evening gown and about her many gifts and talents. I was amused, watching a bit of pride blossoming into a lovely smile as she commented: "it was a joy-filled challenge". For a few more minutes we talked about her nearly magical art form. As we began to roll our mats up, I suggested that we both try one last pose. "Before we start, I need you to repeat FIVE TIMES with conviction: I CAN...I CAN...I CAN...I CAN STAND ON MY HANDS. You can do this. But first... re-wind today's tape to the moment you hung that gown on a hanger and just felt so wonderful and proud. OK, now BE THERE looking, with your inner yogi strength, at that gown.... are you there?"   She nodded.   "Be at one with this wall, this floor and yourself...JUST DO IT LILY!" She took three powerful steps, threw her hands on the floor and her body inverted. "I DID IT...I DID IT...I DID IT," she proudly cheered.   After four more successful attempts, we laughed and nearly cried our way to the parking lot.

"*Conceive, Believe, Achieve*" – Napoleon Hill
I will forever have the above quote emblazoned on my heart. I refer to it on a daily basis.   Three little words that form a blessed and winning triangle.   For me, it's the A, B, Cs of fulfillment and success. For me **Believe** is the most

16

important of these three little words.   For me, it's a fail-safe system. I might dream up a fantastic concept, something that everyone could use.   I can draw it, I can write about it, but if I don't "Believe" in this idea 100%, it won't ever fly...never ever.   When I fall short of believing in my concept...really in myself...I remember to *Transfer my Confidence*. Sometimes I can become so stubborn that I forget about how successful this *Transfer* process can be.   Every so often, I feel like a tire stuck in the snow...spinning around and around and driving itself deeper into the snow.   The only way out is to: "STOP", push the reset button and *Transfer Your Confidence*. Because no one is listening, I can feel free to give myself little pep talks now and then...like: "Oh my God you are such an amazing jewelry designer.   Necklaces, rings, bracelets, earrings... you can do it all with such style and flair: sincerely Kathleen, you are a one-of-a-kind genius". I click my heels three times, slide off of cloud nine and head back to the drawing board, "Believing" in the idea that I just "Conceived".   Now I can be totally about "Achieving" success.

CHAPTER FOUR
Use Your Failures

"You miss 100% of the shots you don't take." – Wayne Gretzky.

How many of you have heard this joke: "Excuse me sir, but how do you get to Carnegie Hall?"   You all know the answer: "practice, practice, practice". Even if becoming an opera diva hasn't ever been on your list of dreams and desires, *Transferring Your Confidence* will begin the process in any venue of your life.   We all hate to fail.   We have just got to realize that failing is simply a part of life. If you haven't ever failed, you haven't ever taken chances. If you haven't ever taken chances, you haven't gone beyond your comfort zone. Don't deny failures; use them. Failures and setbacks are gifts. They add patina to your work. Movies, literature and music all have twists and turns...they make the project and the artist interesting and keep it alive. Failures are simply stumbling blocks, like punctuation in a letter or a book. You might just say one day: "a failure...hooray...that will fit perfectly into my project." Do you think that Picasso planned to put a nose on the side of a face next to an ear? Gaudi was a visionary way before his time. His cathedrals in Spain were not ever set in stone. He continued to learn as he created his masterpieces. His so-called failures ended up being his triumphs.   We never need to fear failure; it makes the winning even more delicious.

Some years back, Oprah invited everyone over 50 in her TV audience to write to her about: "why are you fabulous?". The 18 winners would spend the day in Los Angeles with her and Tina Turner. Can you imagine the LONG list I built about "why I am NOT fabulous"? I was literally down in the dumps with nowhere else to go but up. I flipped that paper over and began to write down attributes that I have nurtured, unique inventions I'd created and values that I've upheld and lived by to this day.   Oh, the top of the list: my outrageous sense of humor. Next, I called my best friend. "Bring your camera over here after work, I will fix dinner. I need some great photos because I am going to be on the Oprah Winfrey Show with Tina Turner!" One week later, the show called me with airfare!   Why concentrate on dreams that haven't come true? Why live under a bridge with the trolls? Why not inspire yourself? Why not have a little chat with your child within and become your own cheerleader. Give yourself a daily pep talk.   Flight attendants suggest: "put your oxygen mask on securely before you put one on your child". In order to be successful at *Transferring Your Confidence* you must first identify your confidences. Self-help books, meditation, exercise and simply hanging out with people you love will...trust me... build up your confidence list, and not in a hollow or temporary or shallow way. At the end of the day, you must "believe" in yourself and in your strengths. Life is a grand adventure, and adventures have mishaps, false starts and breakdowns.

Olympic athletes train for years. Nothing stops them. They are all like Humpty Dumpty... they fall apart... put themselves back together and begin again. The scars become part of their strength. "Get on your mark, get set, GO" ...a playground command we all obeyed. Today, I use that same line to sort of "suck it up" and: *Transfer my Confidence*. It works! It really works!

Every morning, I take a huge vitamin pill. I mean, I swallow an elephant-sized pill! Armed with a glass of water in one hand and that humongous pill in the other, I get on my mark, I get set and I swallow that pill! I don't think the pill would ever go down if I didn't do my little gyration dance every morning. Remember, a sense of humor is at the top of my list of talents and virtues... it's my safety net...if I can't laugh...mainly at myself... life isn't worth the ride. A few nights ago, I was scrolling down the list of shows on TV. My finger landed on a boxing match and I thought: "God in Heaven, we all beat ourselves up so much. I need to boost myself up more and embrace my various confidence arenas so that I can transfer them to new thresholds". "I dare you... I double dare you" is another grade school challenge. If a friend dared you to do something: YOU DID IT! All grown up, I need to dare myself to jump into various unknowns.... knowing full well that failures are a part of the game of life. 60 years later, I'm taking pride through my giggles at the constant sprinkling of "F's" on my report cards.

CHAPTER FIVE
Small Successes Shine

"Only those who dare to fail greatly can ever achieve greatly." – Robert Kennedy

A sense of accomplishment is such a wonderful feeling... for the good of another...even better... for the good of someone who will never find out that "you did it" is the best. Accomplishments... no matter how big or important they may be... REALLY build up one's confidence. When we were kids, we all wanted to "have the credit" for a task well done. Today, when your confidence is strong and you maintain an inner pride, "credit" isn't necessary. In fact, "credit" can diminish your personal rewards.

Way back when, I thought that working at an advertising company would be the coolest job. I didn't have a resume, I hadn't ever actually held a REAL job... but I thought: "how can I have a resume when I've never worked?" I was loaded down with creativity and I knew that I could be an asset to any firm. So, without knowing about *"Transferring my Confidence"*...that is just what I did. I boldly called the president of an international advertising firm and asked for an interview. He enjoyed my banter and sense of humor on the telephone as he suggested that I pick up a couple of magazines while waiting in line at the grocery store, take them home and study the ads. "If you think you can make a few better, do it & bring them back to me... OK kid?"

I was so excited to give this idea a try! I stayed up until the wee hours, drawing, writing and coloring ad after ad after ad. The next morning, I had (to my mind) improved on 35 ads! I slipped the before ads next to my ads in plastic sheets and clipped them into a binder. The big boss was flabbergasted! He hired me on the spot. I was a copywriter at that agency for five years. Walking to the car, I laughed just thinking about so many teachers saying: "you can't read, write or spell... you'll never get a job". One of my favorite print ads was for Mr. Bubble: "Bubble your kids clean: they'll have as much fun getting clean as they did getting dirty".

It isn't necessary to give this "*Transfer Your Confidence*" concept a first try for colossal goals or "I wish I could" dreams. A simple situation is a fine idea to give *Transferring Your Confidence* a try. For instance, every time I make blueberry pancakes, each pancake tends to fill the pan. Believe me, "Transferring my Confidence" helps me to flip them…each time…to perfection. Small successes will shine a glowing light on more difficult challenges and make them much easier to try and… to win! Suddenly, you become a confident person. Without being cocky, confident people are compassionate and attractive and usually willing to help when needed. Today, thinking back on small successful challenges from my childhood, fills me with pride and encourages me to try, try and try again. What a gift to have "wins" from childhood, empower you today!

Recently, I visualized my skinny little girl frame, shivering to death while looking up at the high diving board at our country club. I was not only dared to jump… I was actually double dared to jump off the high board. As I walked around and around the pool trying to find my courage, I gave myself the quickest "you can do this" pep talk. Finally I was ready to climb that scary ladder up to the high board. With an inner combination of pride winning over my fear, I climbed up, looked ahead and I jumped! After that first jump, I was in line to jump again and again and again for the rest of the afternoon with all of the big kids!

Whenever I flip a pancake, I am on that high diving board ready to jump. Hands down, spatula up…clearly I am one heck of a champion pancake flipper! We have all lived through dares and double dares. Scared as we were, today the successes of nearly "winning the gold" way back then started the building of our inner core of satisfaction and pride. Trust me; this *"Transfer Your Confidence"* will set your mind into a clear place where you can wrap your head around exciting possibilities and new passions. No matter how large or small, looking back on our success stories is always good for the soul. That said, today...conquering our grown up "stop gaps", through this process, will open new worlds, adventures and power every time you choose to *"Transfer Your Confidence"*.

As much as we all NEED to "Believe" in ourselves and in this process, we all have moments when life isn't all sunshine and rainbows. These "I've totally lost it" times are all a part of the human element. As long as we can recognize negative emotional vibrations and switch moods before life gets out of control, then "it's all good". If we don't stay there, then down times can become positive learning experiences. Without staying there, we take control of the reins and steer ourselves out of exhausting round and round cul-de-sacs before unpleasant experiences capture our souls and build negative memories in our minds. Sometimes, "the little brat kid" inside pokes her nasty head out... wanting mommy to make it all better. Like tires in the snow, from time to time, we all get stuck. If your tires are digging in the show deeper and deeper... where you just can't seem to kick the tsunami of depression out... maybe get up, get out and move about. Physical movement always works for me. I take a walk or a little bike ride and give out at least five compliments to people on my path. I'm talking about unique and positive compliments. Infused with new found honesty and flattery, I start giving them away as I continue down the road on my walk or ride. Leaving five compliments on my path becomes a deep paradigm shift in my energy...from down in the dumps (like tires in the snow) to up and having a light and happy heart.

CHAPTER SIX
Dealing with Bullies

People skills are such a huge blessing. Although we all have our favorite friends and relatives, getting along with almost everyone all of the time, can be a nearly impossible challenge. As far back as I can remember, dealing with negative or uninteresting people has been one of my most boring and painful games that I hate to play. I've tried to "*Transfer my Confidence*", but in all honesty that circle of love just never gets in motion with loud mouths. Recently, I had an encounter with a friend who loves to talk and talk and talk. It's a vulnerable state for me but, I too have been accused of being a nonstop talker. I do admit to that crime and I'm working on it.   This particular person reminds me of a guy on a practice tennis court. All of the balls are always on his side of the net. With him, it's about: talk, talk, talk…no chance to get an idea or even a word in edgewise. I couldn't find a single confidence to transfer, so I created a new one. I simply listened, laughed, agreed and smiled as this "blabbermouth" went on and on and on and on. Most of what he said was kind of interesting, but when I couldn't put a single thought or response into the game, I lost interest. As I was fighting a losing battle to participate, to add my two cents, a new confidence evolved that I could transfer. I simply sat back, allowing all of his thoughts, ideas and words to flow. I became very relaxed and he loved having the stage.

The more we grow emotionally, the more confident we become. Soon our wellspring of confidences just sort of mow over any negative thinking and life becomes a treasured, light-hearted dance. A keen sense of awareness of our thoughts becomes stronger so that we begin to sense negativity. Animals are incredible teachers. Oh My God.... their senses are so evolved. They know, they feel when their lives are threatened.

My loudmouthed friend didn't threaten my life... but I did allow him to throw me off balance until I let go of my struggle to participate. He always has a lot to say. He just needs a kind, open-minded sounding board. I had a choice: "embrace or erase". Now I am ready to experience the next person who has tons to say. I will be at the ready to "*Transfer my Confidence*" from "fight or flight" to listening and perhaps learning a thing or two. This emotional growth only evolved through me having a little chat with my EGO... letting it be his turn and then his turn again and again. So often we tend to make "mountains out of mole-hills" when in reality, the situation is no big deal.

You might say: "why do I have to: *"Transfer my Confidence"*? Trust me, it makes the game of life easy. The humps and bumps smooth out. Your likability increases. It is a powerful exercise. Just imagine being confident in more areas of your life than you ever thought possible. Today, you may not feel confident at all...a kind of "down in the dumps" feeling.   Think back to your childhood, when mommy kissed your "ouchy" and it didn't feel better. Truth to tell, at the end of the day, we all need to make it better ourselves. Indeed that inner strength builds confidences that will serve you in the future and make you deeply proud. Think back to the playground. Bullies didn't force themselves on confident kids. "Fake it until you make it" is so true.

No one has to know that you are scared to death and shaking in your boots. On the playground, letting go of a ring tied to a rope and swinging over to the next ring was scary as hell until we learned the swinging process. Often, when I feel I just can't let go, I harken back to those rings, visualizing the next ring as I let go of the first ring. Building up a confidence of letting go is as freeing as a bird in flight.

We collect and hang on to so much "stuff". It all becomes a burden. Change is a concept that is here to stay. So "going with the flow" is the only answer. Grasping and clutching onto possessions in order to have power or acceptance is a losing battle. New possibilities are fleeting and if we HOLD ON to anything too tightly, we miss the new and strangle the old.

CHAPTER SEVEN
Going With The Flow

The other day, I was observing a piece of driftwood along the shore. The wood would rest on the sand and then be washed out to the ocean again. Again and again, on to the shore and back out once more it would travel. I "became" that piece of driftwood. It was a marvelous sensation as I felt the in and outflow! "You win a few: you lose a few". At the end of the day, there is joy in knowing that your confidence cannot be shattered as long as you can trust the process and look forward to what lies ahead. Keeping an open heart, mind and hands has rewards that children feel every day. We might not grow in height, but we can grow in depth and stay open to change. So: *"Transferring Your Confidence"* doesn't need to be specific. You can count on five or so venues of confidence... but in truth YOU ARE your confidence. You are your rock. You are stable and still flex-able and open to change.

This *"Transfer Your Confidence"* process came out of a haystack of nearly impossible personal needs. I am going through some health challenges... aren't we all. That, combined with my age (nearly 75) smashed most of my

Confidences into smithereens. In order to "BE" the glowing star atop my holiday tree, I became desperate to dream up a system that would wake up positive possibilities that were either dead or buried under a mudslide of doubt and depression.

Today, I keep a little pie chart close at hand, with my powers of confidence written on each slice. In thinking back through a kind of "Easter Egg Hunt" for my strengths... I found that the great majority of my virtues began sprouting their leaves and wings in early childhood. It is so easy to take for granted the bedrock of one's unique inner strengths...blessings that comfort and carry us through life. As you look back, you will find that your strengths kind of piggyback each other. For example: if you have always been honest, then fairness in games and business will always be a non-negotiable treasured trait. If compassion is on your pie chart, then a kind and understanding heart will be the next piece of your personal winning pie chart. This throwback to my childhood, gives me a better understanding, respect and compassion for children. We don't always give credit to the fascination, curiosity and wonder that continues to sprout every day in the hearts and brains of children. When the opportunity arises, hang out with kids… you will be surprised at their candor, insights and positive energy.

Think about it… toys, cartoons, games, funny papers and even plush animals are made by: ADULTS! We all have a kid inside. Why not "go there" whenever the occasion arises to hang out with kids. Trust me, wisdom and creativity begins in the baby years. "Don't pay attention to them, they're just children." Less true words were never spoken. Kids keep us open, youthful and full of innocent love. Let's all listen to and learn from and respect children!

"When you are worried and cannot sleep, just count your blessings instead of sheep and you'll fall asleep counting your blessings".   Way back when, we'd call big shot kids: "cocky" if they had a false sense of themselves. At the end of the day, deep down inside, our private gratitude for greatness is the only way to go. Shortchanging or denying your talents, will inevitably short change you and your associate's interactions. STOP selling yourself short… that's not the way the world spins. STOP when you find yourself fixated on your shortcomings. "To win: go within". Yup, this *Transfer Your Confidence*" is an inside job. You'll never have to SHARE your pie chart…rather BE your pie chart!

CHAPTER EIGHT
Avoid Judging Others

I asked a coterie of close friends, if they would read the first few pages of this book and see if this simple system could work in their lives. To my great delight, they were happy to "Transfer Their Confidences" and….it worked! One college buddy was asked to speak at her best friend's eulogy. She said: "her husband asked me and so I couldn't refuse…what to say …what to say?" In quiet prayer, she came up with a combination of her friend's outrageous sense of humor and the daily benefit she had growing up and listening to her father's public speaking. "There were over 500 people in the church and I never faltered. I keyed into the most hilarious adventures we had and spared the last traumatic months. I 'Transferred my Confidences' and it worked brilliantly!" Another friend said: "I never thought much about confidence as I had a great deal of confidence growing up. I had two loving parents who made me believe that I could accomplish anything in life. I now realize, after reading your words, that my insecurities were always washed away through my parents unconditional and unfaltering love for me. Indeed, I "Transfer this Confidence" daily in every venue of my life. Thank you for waking up these positive reinforcements my parents instilled in me".

"*Transferring Your Confidence*" can be seen as a leap of faith. This "leap" is about faith in yourself….believing that: "the good, bad and the ugly" of your past, can serve you and only you today. From getting lost as a child, to a trip or two to the hospital to perfect test scores… we can learn from our mistakes as well as our triumphs. Conquering failures and learning tough lessons from insurmountable setbacks always makes your inner core stronger than ever. It's about forgiving yourself, infusing lessons with goodness into your heart and moving on. Very often, geniuses and philosophers fall off the wagon and lose their direction…they are very wise and understand that ups and downs are a part of the human element that cannot be avoided. Safe isn't always safe…it's rather a stagnant way of being, and can paralyze your good spirits and bring you to a nearly hopeless state of mind. Like patina on tarnished silver, imperfections are the perfections of life. Truman Capote once said: "Babe Paley had only one fault: she was perfect. Otherwise she was perfect."

You may start this "*Transferring Your Confidence*" with a list of five positive attitudes. As you begin to work with these virtues, these gifts, you will soon discover and uncover even more inherent strengths that you can awaken and use today. We are all much more powerful and caring than we ever give ourselves credit for today. Try taking a short walk with an empty mind and a smile on your face. "Let go & let God" might be an overused phrase… but it can serve you on this walk. Be honest with yourself, as you walk and have a little ONE ON ONE mini soul search, more inner attributes will begin to surface. Upon your return home, write your thoughts down… your pen will glide across the page…just as my fingers are typing out these thoughts for all of us. Remember: "You can't read, write or spell… you'll never get a job. No one will ever read anything you write". Gotta love those primary grade school teachers. In a positive way, negativity can be flipped like a pancake to reveal a lovely part of your make-up. "Empowered or Devoured"… it's a choice…right? Oh how we beat ourselves up…I ask myself: "WHY"?

Back to school days. I loved loved, loved dissecting a frog in our high school zoology class. God in heaven, he was an ugly creature. But oh my gosh, as I cut his belly open and pinned back on a sheet of foam board, his incredible insides were revealed! From aubergine, to celadon to indigo… the plethora of magnificent colors and shapes were a sight to behold. Honestly, they took my breath away. At some point, we can't help ourselves, we all tend to judge a book by its cover. Before opening hearts, books and even frogs…why not wait for the reveal? The best gift, as we unpinned and closed our frogs down, was that the ugly outside appeared… through new eyes it was beautiful as well. Just like an abalone shell… when flipped over, a heavenly rainbow is exposed. We are all in such hurries for the end of the book, movie or even dinner… when, in truth… the desserts of life aren't always the best parts. Slowing down and taking in the grain of wood on your floor, the veins in a piece of lettuce even a simple drink of water…enhances our virtues and our self compassion. The tortoise and the hare took different paths at different paces and yet they both arrived at the finish gate almost together. Dare to be different. Dare to think and live out of the box. You will discover new inroads to wonder and youthful curiosity.

"Comparison is the death of joy" Mark Twain.
We are all guilty of comparing ourselves and everything to everyone and everything. This comparison ritual began as kind of personality contest in school. Back in the day, we all wanted to be "cookie cutter" shapes, following the leader of

the pack. Acceptance into the "in crowd" was the only goal…no time for personality development or stepping out of the clique box.   How can anyone "*Transfer Confidences*" when we all… without question…had our heads down in the sand while following the leader?   Looking back on our school days, there are a few glimmers of uniqueness and joy found in creating…. anything.   That fear of stepping out of the "row of ducks" takes guts… but…like loaves and fishes… the rewards keep multiplying as our own personal gifts keep growing and we keep paying it forward.

CHAPTER NINE
We Are All Magnets

Last week, my friend Sarah said: "Kathleen, I just did a *Kathleenism*. I ran into our small post office just as the lady was leaving for lunch. "Could you please take these bills, I'm leaving town and they need to go out today". The postal clerk was so gracious. I was so relieved. I thanked her profusely and said: "I'd love to buy you a cup of coffee for your lunch on this cold day". "Kathleen, she was thrilled to death and said: "why thank you…I think I'll buy a latte". I know you give little pockets full of jewels and trinkets away every day. Today, I now understand why. Forget about the postal clerk…I felt so so good…I still have a smile on my face. I even forgot about a family issue I was churning in my mind and stomach. I just said: 'Sarah, get a life' and walked to my car…all smiles".

A good way to find a confident trait is to have a little *tete-a-tete* talk with yourself in the mirror. "I'm really proud of the way I…."   or: "it's always been so easy for me to…" I have a friend who says: "that's what makes horse races". Choosing to believe in and even bet on what we feel is the winning horse, idea, concept or plan keeps us in the game of life.   Just as the Pied Piper led a crowd out of town, we tend to follow the leader, even if we don't agree with their philosophy. More often than not, trends are created for those who don't have any ideas of their own. I like to check out trends and then cherry pick what seems appealing and add it to my own personal style.   "Fitting in while standing out" is a healthy balance. From the closet to the kitchen, incorporating a trend into your take on something new, will give you confidence and a satisfying flair that is all your own.

It is so important to keep your pie of Confidences near and dear to your heart. There are days, when you don't feel confident about anything. Those are the days it's a good idea to refer to your personal pie chart. In time, you will need to start another pie! Soon, there won't be any need to prove yourself. At work, at home… once you prove yourself to that person staring back at you in the mirror…you won't have any need for approval or acknowledgment from anyone. "*Transferring Your Confidence*"… from weakness into strength… will begin to be as entertaining as any game… in fact…it WILL become the best game in town! Honest, earned and well-deserved confidence is so appealing. Give yourself a moment to page through your list of friends. Next, think of the REALLY confident people in your life. REALLY and honestly confident friends are NEVER "in your face" about anything. They simply ARE what they believe in … what they have created… how they have chosen to live their lives. Think about it… they are the BEST kind of people. They also listen…full out…without an agenda. In conversation, you can tell when someone isn't listening. Rather they are waiting to put their two cents into the conversation. Winning, in any game, isn't the most important part of the game. Starting with "the game of life" once you get that there is more to games than winning… you will forever be a happy camper. What a joy it is to let the other guy win.

Look at the people around you. Take an even closer look at your friends. We are all magnets. If you are spending your time, or better put…wasting your time with creeps and ne'er-do- wells…it might be time to buff up your "inner magnet". Click your heels three times and reinvent the way you spend your precious time. We can't re-wind our tapes or delete our actions. Life is full of learning experiences; if something or someone isn't working for you or empowering you…toss that fish back into the stream ASAP.

Save those quiet moments every day and see how it feels to focus on a virtue a day. It's a heaven-sent idea. Virtues like Gratitude, Forgiveness, Generosity, Integrity, Acceptance and Appreciation. They can fill in gaps and connect thoughts. There isn't any reason to be bored being alone. We have so much to weave, to connect, to discover within our own private game of life. The more you love yourself, flaws and all, the more others will love you. Letting love into your heart can be a sort of "shy" thing. It is easier to connect with others when you re-connect with your confidences and acknowledge: "damn, I am good enough to receive love, in fact I am great!" This is the truth, it is by no means boastful. We were all created for greatness. Uncover your unique greatness, go out and make a difference in the world. It will come back 100 fold.

There are a few tricks to pulling weeds out of your flower garden. If you just pull the weed, it WILL grow back. Here are the tricks: water the weed…loosen the weed…water it a little bit more…loosen it a little bit more. Next… gently, very gently and not in a hurry…pull the weed out of the soil. You will extract the entire weed and it cannot… it will not grow back again.

I've always talked in pictures. Images that make my thoughts come to life. Over the years, these pictures in my mind never get old. For example, I imagined that we all started out, for twenty minutes, on a conveyor belt in heaven. We were all sprayed with talents, gifts, virtues, energy and attitudes and then we fell off the belt and landed on this planet. Some of us landed in privilege, others in poverty. That said, each one of us had what we needed to carve out a spot and make a difference. Wishing for more or other attributes, to my mind, is a waste of time. "I want, I wish, if only I had" depletes the heart full of abundances that we all have to enjoy a rich, full and complete life. In this dream, I find that sharing my "stuff of life" increases it 100 fold.

There are so many blessed people around us that are fine examples of how to live the good life. I'm talking about people with serious health issues, people born "on the other side of the tracks", abandoned and abused people who continue to make a difference with their inborn tools.

CHAPTER TEN
Go For It!

Years ago, here in San Francisco, I had the awesome privilege of hearing... in person... through his computer, Stephen Hawking. Words would only limit his accomplishments, intelligence, positiveness and charming sense of humor. He has always been my "spirit animal". Towards the end of his life, he communicated through one muscle on his cheek. When I am worried and I cannot sleep, I think of Stephen Hawking rather than counting sheep. He transferred, shared and continually reinvented his confidences. He never gave up. He never quit. He was born the same day as Einstein and passed on PI Day. That evening, even though I didn't understand any of his theories, he still inspired and continues to inspire me every day. Whenever I begin to feel sorry for myself, just thinking about all those years Stephen spent in a wheel chair, really shakes my cage. He once said: "people need not be limited by physical handicaps as long as they are not disabled in spirit". He truly believed in people making good use of their lives by seeking "the greatest value of our action". Whenever I feel sort of crippled by any one of the unreachable goals on my *shadow list*... I don't stay in that space...it renders me useless. It is so satisfying to *transfer my confidence* on to a shadow kind of weakness and enlighten it with positive energy. "The greater good" is sprinkled with rewards and goodness galore. From self, to family, to country, to the world...lofty goals are the only way to go. When dreams and desires are about others, the universe provides. Stephen never had "great potential"... because when he thought about an idea...he brought it into reality. Here are just a few of his words that I live by: "Remember to look up at the stars and not down at your feet." "Try to make sense of what you see and wonder about what makes the universe exist." "Be curious". "However difficult life may seem, there is always something you can do and succeed at". "Pay no attention to trends; be yourself".

For me "great potential" is kind of a cop out. If you "have it: do it"... or at least start. Being afraid of a possible failure is such a lame excuse...not to give it a go. "Follow the Leader", "Simon Says" and The Pied Piper legends are all games and folklore where you give power to another. When trail riding, if you stick your horse's nose into the tail of the horse in front of you on the path...then your ride is given away to the other rider. "Chances & Change" are an unavoidable part of life. When riding a horse on a merry-go-round, you must lean off the outside of your horse in order to grab a golden ring as you go round and round. I collected pockets full of golden rings on every ride. What a thrill! I remember catching golden rings like it was yesterday. To this day…"taking scary chances" kind-of-memories still get the adrenaline flowing. It's never too late to start building winning memories. Growing up, I was a total tom boy. Many an evening, rather than doing my homework, I would pick pieces of gravel out of my knees. "You will never have pretty legs when you grow up, if you keep getting into mischief on the playground", my mother would order. Today, those scars are my personal badges of courage. "It's never too late" to dream big, take chances and live on the edge.

Back in the school days, school days good old golden rule days, being on top of your youthful power game also put you at the top of the popularity list. Way, way back in the day, nothing was cooler than being popular. In the long run, the best kind of popular kid was full of fun and all inclusive, rather than like the bullies who were full of huge egos and acting like "big men on campus". We are all magnets. Way, way back in the day, attracting everyone into your circle was a daunting experience. When everyone wanted to be "in the IN crowd", Mr. Nice Guy didn't really have a choice. Today, I can only imagine how pop stars and movie stars try to handle the constant crowding around them in circles…when all they want to do is simply to hang out with their own private inner circle or just be solo for a while. No matter what generation, there is a price to be paid for being popular. We all need time to allow "the dust to settle" in our lives and in our minds. Being popular also has its responsibilities. Popular people are born leaders and we all follow the leader. There are "good cop and bad cop" leaders. "Sheep's clothing" can be misleading. Leading by example means you have to be a worthwhile "follow the leader" kind of person.

We cannot ever take our confidences for granted. They are gifts to be acknowledged and need to be nurtured and protected. They can loom large and attract multitudes. Knowing when to stop what can become madness and check in with ourselves is not only a very good idea but a necessary plan. The best thing is that your confidences can grow and multiply. As confidences blossom, shadows diminish. Holding on tight to your talents will strangle your persona and dumb down your goodness. Giving, whenever, wherever, is a profound way to keep popular people humble and happy. Sending a little bit of money off to a worthwhile cause, visiting the elderly, donating possessions to the needy are all sure ways to compound your confidence and impact your surroundings in a positive way. Staying unattached to "stuff" is so freeing and empowering. Recently, I've had two karmic kicks. They were both "stuff" karmic kicks. They happened, when everything was stolen in my life...TWICE! I admit, I am nearly a hoarder. When terribly in-confident, I believed that I was my "stuff"...that people were attracted to me because of my "stuff". Hard lesson to learn: giving of myself, letting go of "stuff" has been filled to overflowing with rewards that I never imagined possible. This joy is not fleeting.

One of America's most accomplished and renowned artists, Georgia O'Keeffe was open and honest with her friends when it came to her insecurities and failures. But she also acknowledged that making bad work was inevitable, and simply a part of the creative process. She once wrote: "the painting of this morning is no good, but I was much excited over it and I know that something will come". Oprah was asked if she had a bucket list. She replied: "I just lean into what I was created for...that is my bucket list".

When it comes to your confidences..."size doesn't matter". Rather, it is the ease in which you play the game of life with your own unique tool box of confidences that matters. Perhaps you can sew a button on to any garment with precise accuracy. Maybe your garden that you started from a mud pile is something to behold. You might be known for writing Thank You notes, including every thought that went into a party or a gift. It's the good intentions, compassion and positive reinforcements towards others…even strangers… that build up your inner core and may add to your list of confidences.

The tortoise and the hare took entirely different routes and ended up at the same spot at the same time. Indeed, variety is the spice of life. Don't get me wrong here, I'd love to sing, speed read and dance… I'm not above wishing I could be an orator, a conductor or an inventor. Whenever wishes begin to crowd my mind, I just see myself on to that conveyor belt and float down to my spot on Earth and begin again.

CHAPTER ELEVEN
Keep Creating

Here is a beetle and an ant story: how profound can that be? Well, ever since I was in grade school, the Egyptian symbol of a scarab has fascinated me. A scarab is a beetle about the size of an almond. A scarab beetle can roll a ball of tar-like substance of dung...double its weight... straight up a hill without stopping. This dung ball becomes food for the scarab's larva. As sculpture and jewels, scarabs created out of precious stones such as lapis and carnelian with hieroglyphics (long life & peace in the next world) carved on the bottoms of the jewels... were set in the Pharaohs tombs. I have always loved the symbolic nature of scarabs. We all love stories of greatness out of small creatures. How about the song:

> "just what made that little ole' ant think he could move that rubber plant, anyone knows an ant can't move a rubber tree plant. But he had high hopes... high in the sky hopes".

Keep on dreaming, keep on wishing on stars, keep your confidence list so powerful that it bleeds over onto your shadow page and gets that list glowing as well. While I have stars on my mind, here is a little process that really works.

Whenever I have an event as a star on my calendar, I make use of it. In my mind, I lasso a point of the star...it happily pulls me out of bed and down the road until the event. If the event gets cancelled, well I made good use of it and dreamed about it for days even weeks. Maybe try to dream up a few tricks and secrets that make your days magical. Your "kid within" can happily help.

When a confidence becomes weak...no worries, another confidence can boost it up. When you find yourself insecure (in-confident) in any arena in your life, continue to have little chats with yourself. Age, health, job, family... can tear you down. So, before it's too late, remember you can fix it. When you feel down, stay far away from the "poor me" pity pot and negative people. Get back to your confidence list and immerse yourself in your secure attributes. They belong to you...use them! When you are in an "UP" state of being, a positive state of mind, make a list of places you love to visit, people you enjoy, and possessions you treasure, even magazines you can lose yourself in. Keep your list close by at all times. You never know... when you might LOOSE IT. Your list is your security blanket.   Have this list close at hand so that you can immediately refer to it... in order to get you back on track before your emotions get WAY OFF

TRACK and you become DERAILED. It's like keeping your gas tank at least 1/4 full... before you need to call AAA. Funny, AAA is just one A away from AA! Both can get you out of trouble and keep you out of trouble.

I tell my students: "keep on painting, writing, sculpting, sewing, cooking... just keep on creating". Don't "round file" what you call "failures". They will come to serve you. It's all good. An idea, a concept, be it large or small, is such an enormous treasure. Before it disappears, write a few words down to hold that thought...that concept in mind. The creative process is fascinating. I feel it is a combination of what you came into this world with, your experiences, your education and how you choose certain elements to form a concept and then...it's all about how you spit it out. The body can be a magnificent tool. Sometimes we simply need to get up from our project and MOVE!!! Concentration is primary to success... that said...small distractions are important to the creative process. Once you have put it in play, your creation will continue to gestate. Sometimes we have no choice but to leave our idea "on the drawing board". Just like plants, we do have to feed our plan. Do you ever talk to your plants... when no one is listening!?! It's not a silly idea to have a little "tete a tete" with your plants and with yourself. I'm having one right now! "Maybe I should delete that entire paragraph". Yesterday, I thought: "You can combine those leftovers and just add some fresh veggies...yes that will work!"

When American Indians participate in powwow in teepees... they move around the circle in order to feel the ritual from all vantage points. It is a very sacred ceremony. The creative process is similar. Moving around a painting, viewing writing from a new space, tasting and re-tasting a pot of goodness in the kitchen...only improves the creation and gives its creator a pat on the "yah done good" back. I never keep my "nose to the grindstone". I realize that if I've worked long hours diligently I might get a star on my collar and an A+ on my report card. What about the "fun factor"? I prefer the second half of the word: diligently...that being gently. Taking a break, being kind to myself, enjoying the time on and off the project makes the process, and the result, a true joy. I'm "all smiles" when I take a look at the clock on the wall and suddenly realize that I have been totally lost in a jewelry design, or painting or these words you are reading right now... for hours.

I find imagination and the creative process to be so rewarding because I never have a plan or a recipe so I have no idea what the results will be. It's like laughing at my jokes more than any audience member even gets it! I hear a lot: "I don't have a creative bone in my body". Oh yes you do... "that bone" is just sleeping on your shadow side. Be your own inner prince and kiss it awake with a *confidence*! Take baby steps... you will be amazed at your hidden creative talents. Growing up, my sister was the musician... I was the artist. A few years ago, she tried a painting class. She was delighted with her paintings... delighted! Why not dare to branch out and try something new... something that you fear. You will succeed. Wander through a museum or an art gallery... you might not be attracted to all of the art... but the experience of   simply looking will conquer your fear of being an artist. Just imagine one of your drawings or paintings ...framed on your wall! My sister has her own gallery and it has brought her unimaginable joy!

CHAPTER TWELVE
It's All Good

Being a mentor is a blessing to the mentor. Teachers gain so much from their innocent "so anxious to learn" students. What a responsibility it is to open the trap door to students' brains and begin to pour ideas into their minds and hearts. It is a win/win situation. The students feed me and impact my *confidences* in such a pure and fresh way. Each time I leave the classroom, I feel so energized. I dream up a concept, bring it into reality and then share it with my students. In the weeks that follow, they take my idea... expound on it, interpret it to make it their own and often they improve it. I've never suggested that I pay the school to allow me to spend time with the kids... but I've often thought about it.

Leaving a project is like a surgeon leaving the hospital in the middle of an operation. In order for success, I need to toss myself into the plan. I must keep all parts of the creation moving and growing. I am like the clown in the circus with ten plates spinning on poles. As soon as one begins to wobble, the clown gets it spinning again. When I get lost in one minute detail, the balance falls off the grid. Once again, I get up and MOVE! Nothing, at the end of the day, is REALLY any big deal. Baby steps and giant steps are intertwined to form whatever is needed. Your inner-self is your best guide.

"From one to whom much is given, much is expected"...Kennedy, Luke the bible &&&... we have all heard this quote in one form or another...from one leader or another. An abundance of spiritual gifts is like a basket of lovely presents. There is a responsibility attached to each gift. With each gift come the tools to use the present and make the world a better place. This may seem like a heavy duty, but it isn't really and the rewards balance it all out to perfection. Another balancing act: the opposite side of a catastrophe. You fall apart. You can't get it together to deal with this horrific event. Here is the balancing act. No matter what the disaster, no matter what the total sadness... there is a gift...the universe provides...right then and there. So, if your house burns to the ground or you break a fingernail...there is a balance of positiveness...right then and there. Be open for it. Use a *confidence*...maybe of strength and trust. If you are rendered helpless, if you are way down in the dumps.... the gift fades away. It's like CRASH: GIFT! I have a friend, who bought a fancy car and wanted to show it to another dear pal. He parked it on the steepest hill in San Francisco. Again, this car was new to him. He forgot to curb his wheels and put the emergency brake on. As he rang her doorbell, he heard a loud noise…the car rolled down Hyde Street and landed on a fire hydrant, just as the door opened. He is a REAL believer. He said: "well, I can't wait to see what the Universe is going to provide for me right now!"

"Need has nothing to do with it". Some things just feel good to have around for your senses to IN joy. Cashmere, fine wine, art, music… when "need has nothing to do with it"…there is only pure, guilt free pleasure. It's like a clearing in the storm or an oasis in the desert. R & R: Rest and Relaxation is a vital part of daily life. Everything settles down and you …like a farmer on top of his ranch, can see clearly where your confidences are and how they can be transferred to your shadows. Accepting that we all have *shadows* is part of the game of life.   "Game's Over" once your life is perfection. Remember, Truman Capote said: "the only thing wrong with Babe Paley was that she was perfect". There is always time for giving and forgiving. What you focus on: increases. We all spend so much time on the Watch and The Wallet and have little time left for Wit and Wisdom. We need to pretend that there are extra Saturdays and Sundays mid-week. We need to play like children. We need to put seriousness on the back burner. We need to play hooky from work. We need to have wellness days. We need to laugh more than we cry...hug more than we shake hands...dance in the shower.

Maybe ask your best friend: "what do you think are... oh maybe two things that I do with ease and well? I'm just curious...and would love to know if your ideas in this field are the same as mine". I think you'll be surprised with your friend's ideas. Your *confidences* list could change and you might just have some new talents added to your list. We do take attributes for granted...thinking: everyone does it this way or that way....NOT TRUE! People count on us because we do some things in a kind of "no problem" way".

CHAPTER THIRTEEN
Imagine

"Little things mean a lot" sung by Perry Como and "High Hopes" crooned by Frank Sinatra. So many lyrics send out "right on the mark" messages. Keep uplifting ones on your playlist. We all know the words to our forever/favorites. Maybe try karaoke singing them in the shower…like Gene Kelly danced as he sang in the rain to be: "happy again".

Here are a few lines of "HEART" by The Four Aces; they will forever lift me up more than a string of exquisite pearls and breath-taking diamonds:

> You gotta have heart
> All you really need is heart
> When the odds are saying you'll never win
> That's when the grin has to start…1st
> You gotta have heart.

"I never listen to the words in songs …I just listen to the melody". That's all well and good, but words can lift your spirits and heal your soul and get you up and running again. From Elvis, to Pavarotti the lyrics combined with the notes can create a paradigm shift in your energy. IMAGINE by John Lennon is the best example of this paradigm shift in any lyrics that I could ever IMAGINE.

This doesn't ever have to be a goal ...but IMAGINE making a positive difference in the world. Many people have done it. Many times, it wasn't a goal, rather an effect of working with *confidences*.   Penicillin, Pacemaker, Post-it Notes, Ink Jet Printers and X-Ray images... just to name a few "didn't mean to invent it" remarkable accidents. We can all make a planned or accidental difference at home, in our communities or anywhere. Like the domino principle, the rewards   "keep on giving" to the giver and the receiver. Eddie Kendrick's: "Keep on Truckin" was at the top of the charts for months. It is such a positive vibe of a song. You can't listen to this tune without feeling "UP".

Laughter is the "Drano®" of the soul.   A good old belly laugh... especially at no one's expense... gets your heart and soul pipes moving... and dancing.   The old saying: "oh just laugh it off" has a lot of truth to it. "I laughed so much... tears ran down my leg".   "Laugh and the world laughs with you". My favorite from Milton Berle: "laughter is an instant vacation". Best truth: laughter is a calorie reducer. Yup, laugh a lot and watch the pounds disappear! Everyone has a unique laughter. Across the room, across the table, it's interesting to listen to laughter. As people change and grow...so does their laughter. Some are full out while others are quite restrained. Over the years, as people quit giving a damn... their laughter changes and it punctuates their lives. Serious events... level the playing field of life. Events and calendars become less important as laughter, joy and appreciation step up to the helm. "Oh, just laugh it off" has a lot of truth to it. The giggles occur at the most unexpected times and events.

For instance, take my mother's funeral. Sounds like Henny Youngman's line: "take my wife.. please"! Just continue on to this "laugh 'til you cry" true story. The family was gathered on one side of the front altar of the cathedral. Just as my mother wanted it, there was a bevy of priests saying mass. She wanted an open casket; with a rosary draped around her hands and a new white robe...kind of angel like ... yes I have my tongue in my cheek right now. A dear friend drove my sons and me up to Portland, Oregon from the Bay Area for the memorial. The alcove to the left of the altar was pretty full. My friend stepped back away from the family allowing everyone to find a seat. Indeed, he moved out of the way...

right on to the temporary pew that wasn't nailed down. The pew toppled over, my friend did a full somersault and nearly landed in the casket with mom! Giggles galore ensued. It was hilarious! We all needed a break from the tissue box passing and the seriousness of it all.   Laughter is so healing and oh so necessary ...every day.

CHAPTER FOURTEEN

Age Doesn't Matter

When it comes to *Transferring Your Confidences*, age is never a factor. When it comes to emotions, feelings and being confident, it's easy to forget how mature the younger generations are. "Don't pay any attention to them, they're just kids"... untruer words were never spoken. Kids just need a balance of discipline and freedom in order to grow and find their ways. We "grown-ups" don't always take the time necessary to acknowledge and appreciate children for their baby steps towards adulthood. They all need time to "talk it out" with adults. They need a safe space, kindness and an ear to be heard. It's a real challenge for a youngster to open up, especially if he or she feels that no one cares. Once they get into the habit of holding feelings deep inside, it is difficult for these precious children to ever open up. Before we busy adults even take time to notice, children's *shadow* sides grow and *confidences* begin to disappear. From the day of planting, espalier plants are trained to grow in patterns against walls and fences. We can all take a note from the "espalier" playbook as we carefully teach and train children to grow with inner beauty and *confidence*. Children, with nurtured pride, will grow up making a difference. From lemonade stands to valedictorian speeches… children will be outstanding and happy if they are given proper roots and flexible wings to fly.

A crutch is only a crutch when it becomes a crutch.   Use it; don't abuse it.

I have a young actor/writer friend who just took up painting. She hasn't experienced a single brush stroke of struggle, rather she is "in total control "of her brush strokes and of her new found *confidences*. She is delighted. Best part, this new creative painting venue is giving new life to her writing and her acting career. *Confidences* are contagious! There isn't anything better than choosing to have your *confidences* bounce off of another one. A flexible *confidence* can be improved upon, adjusted or joined with another *confidence*. In no time you will have a baker's shelf full of *confidence* pies! Like being in the zone of happy and satisfied greatness with your cooking and sharing that yummy success with other *confidences*…like perhaps your organizational skills. Why put limits or stop gaps on your life? As the kids say: "hello, it's your life, isn't it?"

CHAPTER FIFTEEN
Nothing Is a Big Deal

A flying buttress is an arched support to help support heavy walls… like walls of cathedrals. From time to time, we all nearly fall apart before remembering that we do have inner support. Imagine operating without a skeleton, emotional strength and our amazing brain power. "I want my mommie to make it all better" is a cry that will never be answered. Falling apart is 100% OK as long as we put ourselves back together as soon as we realize that we've lost it. Our individual flying buttresses are available in many forms. Psychologists, psychiatrists, preachers and priests can help to get us up and running. Close friends and "self-help" books are also there when needed. Sometimes medication can be helpful. Whenever we feel like we are going on a side way track to nowhere, above all our *confidences* are the most reliable and quickest cures. Never forget: there isn't a rule that says you can't be your own best friend!

People pleasing and over compensating…in order to be accepted, appreciated and loved… simply does not work. Actually, there isn't an "in order to" that works. The hair goes up on the back of our necks whenever we feel that someone is trying too much "to get in". For sure and guaranteed, that kind of chatter will always result in negative reactions and results. If you feel like you are being judged or slighted, it is a concentrated challenge to stay real, to behave naturally and to "move on down the road". More often than not, our imaginations go crazy and need to be reeled in. No one can like you more than you like yourself. Whenever we feel we are way off our centers, a paradigm shift in our thinking, the sooner the better, can avoid lasting scars and will for sure, tear down shadows and build up our own personal flying buttresses. Personal perfections are lofty goals. Perhaps, happiness and a giving heart are more realistic and attainable goals.

Every so often we all find ourselves…"Grasping at Straws" like a drowning man trying to save himself…even by grasping onto a floating piece of straw. In stillness… best "to win/go within". Here is my theory about someone drowning yelling: "HELP ME, HELP ME!!" : I throw a rope out to him saying: "grab one end and toss it back to me…I'll get you out". Then, I wrap the rope around a tree and toss the other end back to my friend. "Wrap one end around your waist and pull yourself out with the other end…I'll be here cheering you on." At the end of the day, we are our best source of salvation of winning of staying afloat. Indeed, at the end of the day… "it's always an inside job". Think about your friends and family; we all prefer to hang out with positive, confident people who know how to make use of a sense of humor."Is the glass half full or half empty?"   "I don't know, but it's enough for me" kind of humor that will catapult you out of any stressful situation. We can all afford to keep our laughter "at the ready"…starting with being able to laugh at life in general… it really levels the playing field from steep hills and deep valleys of the soul. Choose to say: nothing is "a big deal'.

CHAPTER SIXTEEN

Stay Open

The other day, a dear, wise and entertaining friend expressed a few thoughts to me. "I don't ever want to take any part of my life for granted". He continued: "my life is so wonderful, I just don't want to get used to anything…so I mix it up a bit. I take different roads home, I change my diet, I stay away from getting in ruts by avoiding doing the habitual activities. Most importantly, every day, I stop and gratefully wonder about the world around me as I pinch my sleeping mind awake". With a sweet smile on his face, he said: "tickling is fascinating; you laugh but it hurts and you can't tickle yourself. We are social beings. We need each other…to bounce ideas off of and to tickle! I just find that interesting." This friend is nearly 90 years old and is still totally delighted to be alive. Lastly he said: "I take every day as a gift. I give back to anyone and everyone… some people say they 'pay it forward'. Maybe I can impart some history, wisdom and "can do" positive energy on to younger generations".

I call it my "PUSH" theory. As I leave the bank, the juice bar, the gym…I see the word PUSH on the door. Just for serious fun, I decided to always say: "Pray Until Something

Happens". I use it daily, as I PUSH a door open on to the world. I expect surprises, I'm open for miracles, and I find joy on my path. Another fun self-made-custom: whenever I get change from a purchase, I toss the pennies out into the parking lot. The finders are keepers of a bit of magic and I break into a child-like kind of smile.

"That's what makes horse races" my pal says whenever she notices how different we all are. "Vive La Difference"... is her mantra. She firmly believes that we were not put on this earth to be clones. As Cezanne said: "he who follows is always behind". Copying art, recipes, and stories is all well and good as a learning experience, as long as we learn and then create. I've never found much reward in copying anything. I even mix up a joke to make it my own. Most nights, when my kids were young, I'd tell them bedtime stories in fresh, sometimes scary ways. Even though a story might be a winner, even though a menu might be close to perfect...still... getting out on a new limb is worth the effort. "Tried and True" is a safe winner, but something exciting and innovative is good for the mind and taking chances is so invigorating.

We all hated our school uniforms. From class pictures, to parents' days, we couldn't stand to look alike every day. Once a month we'd have "free dress day", and we all loved it! Everyone had an opportunity to express themselves. The day before free day, creativity soared throughout the classroom. We all felt like paper dolls, dressing ourselves up for a day! That evening, we lived in fantasy worlds, picking out "a look" in our closets to express the mood we had chosen for the day. From risqué to high style mode... whatever our hearts desired, we were all fashionistas for a day. I few of our *confidences* came into play that day. It took guts to wear combinations that were fashion risks. We were all quite daring and innovative. Be it casual or a pretend magazine cover girl, we all twirled throughout the day.

Something to look forward to on our calendars is so important. We all have "a kid inside" who wants to have playtime...all the time. Even if a scheduled event is canceled, we still enjoy daydreaming about the party... that's half of the fun. Gift wrapping is half of the excitement and thrill of what's inside of the package. Again, giving and receiving are equal energies. Just watch the giver as the receiver opens the gift. Both friends are thrilled!

Your list of *Confidences* won't ever dissipate or fade out of existence. The list will remain strong and still...the list can grow. Being open and optimistic is the key here. It's so wonderful, when you embark on something new, that you leave fear in the back seat and to your surprise... you love the activity!   Best part of this scenario is that you are good, in fact great at it! Holding out for flawless perfection on any project is worse than jamming your brakes on and becoming stagnant, motionless and completely helpless. Even if you didn't win the gold, put a star on your collar or an A+ on your report card, give yourself a well earned bear hug kind of pat on the back for trying. Competition is fierce out there. Don't beat yourself up for being average... don't forget average starts with an "A"! Being an inner critic, while beating yourself up is such senseless behavior. We are all vulnerable and that negative energy can have a pernicious effect on our subconscious positive energy and can render us useless.

In regard to our flaws, mistakes and shortcomings, once you recognize that you are forming mental habits of being excessively hard on yourself, you need to quiet those thoughts and press the delete button. Immediately, get back to your *confidences* list and "BE" in your own state of

71

happiness and success. Back pedaling is so exhausting and it is so difficult to reverse to begin moving forward once again. On the other hand, immersing yourself into a *confidence* venue is so uplifting and energizing. The time flies by and you get into a flow like a bird in flight. The trick, the real talent here…before it's too late, is to be keenly aware of "wazzup" so that you can choose whether to move forward or clean up your act and begin anew. A test of real *confidences* is the absence of a need for flattery. Success is all the flattery you will ever need. Then compliments and praise are icing on the cake.

Being real and truly authentic, mostly to *yourself*, is a reward all unto itself. Remember that imposing, scary wizard in The Wizard of Oz? Remember when Dorothy's little dog, Toto wondered and sniffed his way behind the imposing wizard's moon face? There he was… a little bully of a tiny guy. Hands down, that blowhard of a coward lacked confidence and all of the virtues like compassion and humility that are a part of having *confidence*. Self important, boastful egotistical human beings are sort of: "shopping for what they don't want". Why would anyone strive to be cocky, the leader of the pack or the big kahuna of any gang. "Follow the Leader" is not a game I am ever up for when I can nearly smell a stinking

"WIZARD"! Fairy tales are sweet and scary at the same time. Life Lessons from *The Wizard of OZ* like: "have courage" and "all you need is the right inside of you" have been teaching children and adults how to be human for over 75 years.

CHAPTER SEVENTEEN
Little Things Mean a Lot

Think of a handful of foods that you love to eat. Now, in your mind, breathe in as you sense the taste, smell and texture of each divine delicacy. How do you feel? (Stick with me here for a minute). Next: take a look at your list of five *confidences*. BE inside of each one. I promise you, being enveloped by your FIVE FAVE FOODS and your *FIVE CONFIDENCES* will reward you with the same FANTASTICLY SATISFIED MOOD.

We all think of: "taking it for granted" in different ways. Let's give our *confidences* a go and see if we are "taking them for granted". They need acknowledgement. They need nurturing. They especially need to be used and shared. Whatever you are naturally good at... well----> USE IT! Give your blessings, talents and gifts a place to grow and make a difference in the world. Making others' paths smoother, giving a hand...even if it isn't required or requested...will give back to you a hundredfold. If you feel a sense of fear or trepidation when making use of a   *confidence* on your list... then you are not confident about it. Keep it on your list... soon it will become tried-and-true. The first time I tried to drive a stick shift car, I nearly lost it as did my father. Towards the end of his lesson, a combination of his patience and wisdom and my "can do" attitude... the car began gliding back home. From that day on, I was an expert "shift car" driver. Some *confidences* don't start out with a "falling off a log" kind of "know how". Like riding a bike, falling off the bike is part of the learning how to stay on and ride a bike. Look around your life and your surroundings. What are you unknowingly "taking for granted"? You don't have to click your heels and go back to Kansas... just keep your heart and your eyes wide open and appreciate the simple and magnificent experiences and "stuff" in and around your life.

The pendulum swings. From time to time, you too will dip way down and then swing up again. As Joseph Campbell believed, we all experience "departure, fulfillment, and return". Believe in this process... it's one of the most natural flows of life...so why not enjoy the ride. We all have "woulda, coulda, shoulda" lists. Why relive unpleasant experiences. UR where UR right this moment. There will be many more moments... perhaps choose for them to be good and memorable. We can all choose to wipe resentments & regrets off the chalk board in our minds. They do not serve us. They are anchors that keep our boats from sailing into a wonder filled future.   If a moment isn't what "dreams are made of" and you know it…beyond a lesson, don't linger there. Acceptance as to where you are right now and having willingness to stay or move ahead has powerful results. "At the end of the day, we are all in this together". Or perhaps a better idea: "at the end of the day, we're all in this alone". Here is a third try: a combination of together and alone: a sort of WE/ME venturing out into the unknown. Sometimes we do the WE part of life too much and become a victim or play the "blame game". This is the time to turn your "WE" upside down and spend more time in a "ME" frame of mind.

Many years ago, a dear friend said to me:"I have a "TL" for you". "What is a TL?" I questioned. "Oh it means Trade Last. Growing up in Connecticut, we all had a happy habit of sharing 'TLs'. So, if I hear someone saying something sweet, positive or kind about you…then I have a "TL" for you. Here is the deal: right then and there… you are put on the spot and have to give a "TL" a Trade Last to your friend before she tells you what someone said about you". So, it's always your turn first. It's a given, that from out of nowhere, I'm about to hear something flattering about me. The immediate "on the spot" challenge here is that I have to either remember something that someone said about my friend or I

76

have to dream up a compliment. "On the spot" compliments sort of run the gamut from something I actually heard or something that I feel. I can either say something like: "you have pretty blue eyes" or, "the other day at lunch, my pal said that you are the most generous person she has ever met". This "back and forth" interaction is an absolutely wonderful, full circle kind of social interaction. Ever since I first heard of a "TL", I have been re-routing positive reinforcements to the people that were mentioned in other conversations. To my mind, that is a "top drawer" kind of habit."TL" interactions will...for sure...boost your entire confidence pie chart. Now days, in my heart, I jot down compliments that will become "TLs"...and best part...I'll receive one in return...last!

"You are such a phony", an acquaintance once said to me. I smiled and replied: "sorry you feel that way about me... this is my only act and it's me, so I can't go back to being real...this is me. This is real"! Getting engaged in a "gossip fest" will build up your shadow side and shrink your *confidences*". In the long run, gossiping is not cool. As the conversation ensues, any kind of "feel good" attitude disappears and weakens our inner core. You'll never see a confident and kind person in a gossip circle.

CHAPTER EIGHTEEN
Why Me?

I found myself judging a few people this past week. A lady in church… a friend in yoga class… a guy at the market. Three strikes and I was out. Yup, I was out and feeling pretty ugly. "Was that me judging those people"? Indeed it was me. Time to teach myself a strong, and much needed, lesson. Judging another stops any possibility of appreciation, acceptance and discovering truths that lie just below the surface of all of us humans. My biased opinion needed to be replaced with openness. "Judge and you will be judged". It's also a benchmark as to how I'm feeling about myself. Daily self acceptance is imperative. Don't be afraid to check in with yourself and check out your assets. A *confidence* can dissipate and fade away. Like a farmer, checking to see that all of his livestock are healthy and happy, more often than not, we too need to say "hello, how are you doing?" to that person staring back at us in the mirror. A life of "*Transferring Your Confidences*" is no cakewalk. You will continue to have a winning, richly rewarding life if you dare to keep your *confidences* on track.

"Why Me?" is such a waste of time and effort. Remember the conveyor belt in heaven analogy? Basically, you have everything necessary to live your best life. If you feel out of sorts, check your *confidence* list, get in touch with a really good and honest friend or take a nature walk. Mini meditations are also God sent. Simply taking three deep, empty minded breaths will do wonders for your spirit and good will. Meditation is so individual. Some people like to walk on the beach, breathing in and breathing out, while keeping an empty, stress free mind. Others find it a meditation, simply riding a bike on a country road. For focus of my wandering mind, I prefer an image in my meditation. Lately, I imagine a gray pearl atop my belly button. As I breathe out, the pearl grows and grows into a large rainbow colored balloon. As I breathe in, the balloon downsizes back into the gray pearl. The deeper I breathe, the more the balloon grows. This process lasts until I feel complete, clear headed and refreshed.

Back to my report cards, punctuated with Ds & Fs. Other than art classes, an A or a B on a test or report card was as rare as a perfect sand dollar found on the shore. One afternoon, after flunking a Homer's Iliad test, I wondered up a grassy knoll above school where I sat down to read the

Odyssey. As I turned each page, I had to reel my mind back to the book. With dog eared and highlighted pages throughout the book, I headed back down the hill and tried to remember the story I had just read.   That evening, I figured: "what do I have to lose? I'll just go for it and write an outrageous paper". I got into my often child-like wandering mind and began to write my paper.   With pen in hand, I wrote a story comparing Odysseus to a "trick or treater" as he wondered home from Troy along the coast of the Adriatic Sea. Some strangers took him in and comforted him while others turned him away. To my surprise (and I'm sure to the surprise of my Humanities professor) a got an A+ on the paper! Often, when you just can't "go by the books" or "color within the lines"…it's time to be outrageous and make a statement that is a joy to behold. Fifty plus years ago, with a huge tickle infused smile on my face, I still look back on Odysseus "trick or treating" his way home. Happy memories are so nurturing for your child within and the charming adult that is you!

For special occasions, I've never been known to haphazardly grab anything out of the closet and toss it on. That's not "the way I roll" into an event of any kind. When I head out the door to greet the world, I'm most comfortable if

I choose to express the way I feel, what story my "look" will expose, the atmosphere and the other guests at the event. A little chat in the mirror might be called for here. "OK, little girl, what are you going to wear today?" A "look" can expose intelligence, humor, creativity and of course a silhouette. Your history can remain a mystery, but why hide your story: the real you? When you feel you have nothing to hide or to loose, the way you twirl or catwalk or sneak into an event becomes your primary magnet. You will attract like minds and engage in intriguing and interesting conversations. Relying on and trusting your *confidences* is so freeing and exciting. There is nothing to alter or be ashamed of. You are you and that is that!"

Many mindful psychologists believe that it takes 21 days to make or to break a habit. Making and breaking are both concentrated efforts of desire and steadfastness. *Transferring Your Confidences* can really come into play here. Inner core *confidences* will keep you on track as you keep your goal in mind. If you choose to, this can be an entertaining and rewarding three week period. It's like a crash course where you are the student and the teacher... where cheating or lying to yourself won't work. On your computer or on paper, set the 21 days up with a positive message written down on each day. Be your own coach and cheerleader. Applaud yourself. Feel proud. Talk fears away. Daily, believe in yourself and this project. Stay away from excuses and negative energy. Begin the countdown on the first of the twenty one days. Maybe even plan a little celebration with a best friend, or your *very* best friend…that person looking back at you in the mirror. Along the way and especially on day 22, there will be temptations to slide back into your old habits. This is a time when your *confidences* can support you like flying buttresses. Keep a few mantras on paper around your room, in your car …everywhere. "You did this". "You crashed through your own glass ceiling"! Remain optimistic about staying the course in regard to this WIN!   Be your own very proud personal hero.

Addictions are situations we all hope to avoid. Having been a painter for most of my life, I know that when you mix many colors together, even when you are cleaning your palette… brown is the muddy color that the mix makes. I just realized that brown is also the color of many addictions. For instance: tobacco, many spirits, cola and chocolate are all brown in color… as is the color of mud and dirt. Farmers recycle their livestock's "big potty" by mixing it with dirt… and you know what… the mixture of "dirt & dung" is the best fertilizer for planting seeds. Indeed, the seeds are nurtured and grow most healthy in this "dirt and dung" combination. We can all use this analogy if we or someone dear to us, falls prey to and is nearly swallowed up by an addiction. Before it's too late, an addiction, a muddy life... can possess you unless, just in the nick of time, you conquer it with tremendous zeal. Once again, you have a *confidence* that can come to your rescue to defeat an addiction. Just as a farmer plants seeds in "dirt and dung"...you too can find new life as you learn from the dark shadow of an addiction and let it go.

A few weeks before I was going to teach painting on a cruise to China, I had to be rushed to the hospital. My memory all but disappeared. I was suffering from a temporary disease called Trans Global Amnesia. It only lasted for a few hours. Fast forward two weeks: my records traveled through our hospital and the afternoon before I was to leave for China, I received a call from our local Oncologist. "You need to come to my office tomorrow". I replied: "sorry I cannot come in, I'm leaving for China tomorrow morning". In a very direct and emphatic manner he demanded: "you aren't going anywhere tomorrow except my office...you have blood cancer and I need to get you on chemo immediately". My heart sank. I felt like I was going to the principal's office for a crime that I didn't commit. I began unpacking and taking photos of each outfit, thinking I'd go on a cruise to China soon. As I was putting my clothes away, I glanced at my computer and saw that I was invited by Woody Allen to audition to play the part of Alec Baldwin's mother in the movie *Blue Jasmine*. The following afternoon, I started on four chemo pills a day and headed into San Francisco to the audition. As we walked through Chinatown to my agent's office, I said to my husband: "OK this has been a crazy 24 hours". I had to dig deep inside my heart to unearth my sense of humor. Thank God, that *confidence* is always "at the ready" for me. I messed up the read. (They later cut the part out of the movie anyway). We headed to my favorite lunch spot for a burger and fries. I decided, that day to be grateful, to feel blessed and to know there were many joys just around the corner. I've never taught art on a cruise to China and that is all right. "If you keep your head down looking at the cracks in the sidewalk, you will miss the butterflies." Choose to say: "it's no big deal". I did just that.

"Fear is not an option" are the words that Diane von Furstenberg lives by today and Learned from her mother Liliane, a holocaust survivor. At 22 years old and weighing 49 pounds, Liliane told her captors at Auschwitz "I am in excellent health". She refused to be a victim. Indeed, Diane has taken up her mother's mantle with great pride and compassion. She credits her success to her mother's strong will, which in turn, gave Diane the strength necessary to live a fulfilling and generous life. These "DVF" sound bites are words we can all learn and live by: "Be yourself. Be authentic. Be in charge of your life. When you doubt your power, you give power to your doubt. Find the tools needed to live the life you were meant to lead". I'm sure that Diane lives her *confidences* and "stares down" her shadow side until it disappears. People in the fashion world say she is so open yet focused, entertaining yet determined, unafraid yet vulnerable.

CHAPTER NINETEEN
Happiness

OK, let's get back to being happy. From Pharrell Williams' "Happy" to Bobby McFerrin's "Don't Worry, Be Happy", everyone can choose from a myriad of happy songs and karaoke the words--in the car, the shower…anywhere. Like a child blowing out all of the birthday candles and believing that wishes and dreams will come true, we too…through Happy songs…can have an immediate 180 degree mood swing. You could stay down in the dumps, but that area is always overcrowded with unhappy people. Being full of doom and gloom has no future. Like turning a light switch on with just a click, you can turn your frown upside down and BE HAPPY: NOW!

I was happily surprised to see that there is an international summit called "The World Happiness Report". The top countries that scored highest numbers were judged by six of the key variables that have been found to support well-being: income, healthy life expectancy, social support, freedom, trust and generosity. Happiness is now considered appropriate for study at the university level.   A class in the psychology of happiness is sold out at Yale; The University of California at Berkeley has a whole department devoted to the science of happiness.

The anti war slogan of the '60s: "Make love, not war" might not be feasible for the greater part of the population, but "STOP WARS" was clear. From the Bible to the U.S.Constitution, we all hope for and pray for peace. Serenity and a tranquil way of being seems so simple, but just as quieting the mind seems easy, so to... we can allow goodness to be interrupted. Indeed, it takes courage to stand up for what is right, honest and the truth. Tempers can flair; patience can become impossible and just being a nice person can be pushed to the back burner...forever! Maybe if we all incorporated: "Do unto others as you would have them do unto you" every moment of every day, the world would become a HAPPY place. Competition can be healthy and it can destroy. If a game or a job has positive expectations for all, then the outcome will be a WIN for all. Maintaining an optimistic positive attitude, NO MATTER WHAT, will make your life beautiful.

From Shakespeare to Einstein, there are so many remarkable people who have graced our planet and left it a better place for all of us. That said, let's give a bit of thought and a shout out to Dr. Seuss and Mr. Rogers. They weren't afraid to be thought of as sissies. They both had a mission to keep children safe, infused with love, creativity and pure joy. And let's give credit to these two men for keeping their child within alive, well and HAPPY. Their child-like innocence was nothing short of pure magic. Both attended Dartmouth. Dr Seuss went on to Oxford.

Mr. Rogers:

> When I was a boy and I would see scary things in the news, my mother would say to me, "Look for the helpers. You will always find people who are helping."
> Play is often talked about as if it were a relief from serious learning. But for children play is serious learning. Play is really the work of childhood.
> Knowing we can be loved exactly as we are gives us all the best opportunity for growing into the healthiest of people.

Dr. Seuss:

> Today you are you! That is truer than true!
> There is no one alive that is you better than you!
> Don't cry because it's over.
> Smile because it happened.
> You have brains in your head.

You have feet in your shoes.

You can steer yourself in any direction you chose.

We are built to be social beings. It's a psychological fact that people, from childhood and into adulthood, who have a coterie of dear friends... are found to be happier, more grateful and naturally connect with others more easily. True friends have stood the test of time with each other... they have been there for each other's ups and downs ...wins and losses and only love one another more through struggles and shared successes . In the "day to day long run", happiness isn't just about positive emotions or feeling good. Rather, it is an ability to handle difficulties in life by making use of your *confidences* and also.... in choosing to live a meaningful life. Academic and business achievements are all well and good...at the same time... self care and well-being need to grow and be acknowledged as well. Back in the day, "bookworms" were notability clumsy when it came to social interaction. During those school days: "all for one and one for all" didn't happen too often, and the odd man out was usually the "bookworm". Being shy is a "real bear" to conquer... but it can be done. Recognizing and making use of your *confidences* and overcoming your fears...your shadow side... will be your best support in finding and having a happy life with "your" people. Kindness, generosity and understanding are perfect starters and can easily be learned. Giving honest compliments also opens social doors. Empathy is also golden. Being empathetic means that you REALLY feel another person's pain and suffering. For instance: if someone is struggling, you are there for that person...you empathize with them. Sympathy, on the other hand, is a different kind of bird altogether. You recognize situations and feel sorry for people going through challenges and sorrow, but you don't dive deep with them in caring and empathetic manners.

It's in our DNA to be caretakers. Look at primates...they care for and protect their young and the elders in their families. They too are social beings. "I just don't go out too much, there are too many germs and scary people around these days". Trust me, staying alone in your room... while there is a parade outside to enjoy... just isn't going to bring happiness into your life. Even if you are shy and nearly afraid in public, surely you have a *confidence* or two on your list that can be incorporated into your life in order to dissipate your shyness and replace it with a gracious and likeable presence. Remember, we humans are social beings. Transfuse your *"brilliance confidence"* (you have it ... don't

SHY away from it) into your shy little world and get ready to experience a whole new world of joy and giving. You can birth the excitement of being a child every day. Even if at first you feel a need to fake the adrenaline rush that comes from being excited... you will find a way to BE that kid in the candy store! You will cease to be afraid of joining in on a conversation, a game or even simply hanging out and IN-joying the easy company of others.

CHAPTER 20

Be True To Yourself

Independence, dependence and interdependence are all valuable social norms... as long as there is a healthy balance between you and all three "dependences". As adults, it's best to begin with independence... that is the knowing you can be self-sufficient...no matter what. Dependence is all well and good as long as you don't begin to lean on something or someone so much that you become weak and needy. Interdependence is a lovely state of being where the best parts (the *confidences*) of each individual make the whole group happy and grateful. Lady Gaga started out on the road of life as a shy person. She began to burst through her shyness by believing in herself and sharing her thoughts. Here are a few:

> Don't you ever let a soul in the world tell you that you can't be exactly who you are.
>
> Well that's your opinion, isn't it? And I'm not about to waste my time trying to change it.
>
> If you don't have any shadows you're not in the light.
>
> I've been searching for ways to heal myself, and I've found that kindness is the best way.

I am my own sanctuary and I can be reborn as many times as I choose throughout my life.

I feel like you're a really good human being, you can try to find something beautiful in every single person, no matter what.

I allow myself to fail. I allow myself to break. I'm not afraid of my flaws.

Whether I'm wearing lots of makeup or no makeup, I'm always the same person inside.

Music is one of the most powerful things the world has to offer. No matter what race or religion or nationality or sexual orientation it has the power to unite us.

For years, Socrates' words: "The unexamined life is not worth living" have impacted my life in such a profound way. Seeing as he was born in 470 BC and these words are still quoted... I will forever continue to examine my life by taking a hard, honest look at how I spend my days. Here are a few of my "examination" questions...self to self.

If most likely the result won't amount to much, is it worth the effort?

Is "this" really what you want to be doing? Have you been giving and forgiving?

Does what people think influence your ideas, passions or decisions?

Are you on a road to nowhere?

What accomplishments, in regard to family, career and charities, are you most proud of today?

Then I take a look at my diet, exercise program, sleep and spiritual path to see if any adjustments are needed. I can't lie to myself here anymore than I can hide a box of candy from myself!

I could have a "shrink" or a best friend who could help me to examine my life. Here's the thing: the truth is the truth. No one knows anyone better than they know themselves. From a confession to a pat on the back... at the end of the day, everyone is one's own best critic, audience and best friend.

A best pal, with an open mind and a kind heart, is a genuine gift. Sometimes a bit of guidance or advice might be asked for. Sometimes nothing needs to be said or asked for. There is a *confidence* in having a best pal. It is an honor that must be honored.

To protect and enhance your *confidences*, maybe fill yourself to the brim every day with these FOUR THINGS FOR FREE: 1:AIR... 2:WATER... 3:EXERCISE... 4:SLEEP. Breathe consciously and deeply with an empty mind every morning and evening. Carry a container of water around remembering that we are 60% H2O. Exercise...daily or a few times a week. It will improve your quality of life. For concentration and productivity, try to "stack ZZZZs" at least 7 to 8 hours a night. I don't know anyone who takes total advantage of these FOUR THINGS FOR FREE. The human body and mind are the finest combination of tools in the world. This combination deserves to be cared for with excellence and appreciation.

CHAPTER 21

Go Through It/ Grow Through It

This is a very unpleasant subject, but needs to be addressed: why is it that, from time to time, we get caught up in toxic people and their lives? No one else is responsible for our happiness or our truth. But, toxic people do have negative power. They can be insensitive, narcissistic and even abusive. Whenever we discover that we are wrapped up in toxic people's lives, it is time to delve into our *confidences*, finding our power and "BEING" the strength that can move us up and away from toxic people. "Don't let the bad guys get you down". Stay strong. Get back to your course. Don't allow toxic energy to weaken your life.

Whenever I say to myself: something good is going to happen today...invariably a happy moment or two happens. As children, we all heard a teacher or a parent say: "turn your frown upside down". I never paid attention to this command. I let those five words fly over my head. As an adult, I am taking them to heart. Even when I am sad, a smile is a positive way to maneuver through sadness. The most iconic image of the Buddha is surely him sitting silently under a tree, with his eyes half-closed, while beaming the most beautiful, kind and understanding smile ever.   From deep down inside, an enduring smile can keep you on the sunny side of the street...even in stormy weather.

Many of the tombs in Egypt have been unearthed and ancient magical treasures have been discovered. When Egyptologists think they have uncovered every site, another site is found.   When push comes to shove, when you have no choice but to step up to the plate...there is a very good chance you too will discover a treasure, a power, a new found sense of   wonder about yourself.

When it comes to growing and discovering new venues of excellence within, it is an amazing event. Believe me, in life ..."the fat lady" is and always will be... just tuning up. You might think that you are slowing down, but there are still many more lessons to learn and to share. As you continue to keep a sense of wonder and curiosity alive and "WOKE" you will continue to fill your net with butterflies. Like icing on a cake, when we are satisfied with ourselves, everything is a pleasure; needs and wants will disappear.

Recently, I was looking at my list of *confidences* and my shadow list. To my surprise, without knowing it, I had conquered some shadow wishes and wants and they jumped over on to my *confidence* list! Lately, I've been letting down my guard and talking some of my fears away. When I allow my guard and fears to take over the steering wheel of my life, I will inevitably hit a road block. Sometimes I just sit and pout, until I realize: "hey, this is my life...I am in charge here!" As the kids say: "it's all good". My shadow list is full of impossible desires. Just as "The Man of La Mancha" dreamed the impossible dream... some impossible dreams can become reality. Who would have thought that 18 out of 38,000 requests to spend the day with Oprah and Tina would be a dream of mine that came true!?! I continue to learn from each desire...each shadow... as I kind of "love them and let them go" ritual.

Brave is a magical Pixar cartoon about a girl who faced her fears with courage. Fairy tales and cartoon are full of lessons. Like children, we are never too old to learn. Forever, the innocence of a child is a virtue to keep and safeguard. Santa Claus, The Easter Bunny, The Tooth Fairy are all magical characters that kept us full of wonder and happiness. As adults, it is important to keep wonder and happiness alive. Funny, but many times in our youth, we were punished by actions that have made up who we are today. From teachers and parents, we all endured our share of two words: GROW UP"! I hated to disappoint, but I never REALLY grew up. I'm proud to say, I still haven't GROWN UP! A shadow list doesn't have to be a compilation of insurmountable goals, nor do *confidences* need to be huge. Small accomplishments and doable desires are the makings for positive lists for a positive life.

CHAPTER 22

It's Never Too Late

So often, those over 65 hear: "aren't you too old to try that"?
It's like saying: "I see a rocking chair over there in the corner,
wouldn't you like to sit there?" If you can get out of bed and
brush your teeth… you simply are not too old to venture out
of your comfort zone and discover new joys and creative
endeavors. Whether it's a tried and true *confidence* or
something new…why not give it a go; it's never too late to
take a stand, make a statement or face your fears and watch
them disappear. Yup, it's time to give a shout out to "The
Geriatric Generation." In the words of Aretha Franklin…
show them a little RESPECT! They are all far from "over the
hill". Their *confidences* are ingrained into their lives. The 70+
crowd feel that it's never too late to take a look at their
shadow lists…their "old timers" bucket lists. In the Golden
Age of Life, inventions are still made, recipes are still created
and fresh ideas are still being discovered by retired people. I
call it: "refirement". Older people are wise. Older people are
soothing, understanding and of good council. Older people
are entertaining and great fun. I know whereof I speak: I AM
ONE!

Karl, Mick, Donna, Martha, Barbra are all well into their 70's and are far from being thrown under the bus or (not to be rude) into the dirt. Older people have tried and true life styles that are happily shared. In a safe and secure manner, when fear is considered and worries of days gone by are still present, older people take control and enjoy the adrenaline rush of venturing out beyond their comfort zones. At a certain age, what have you got to lose? Being complacent and rigid might seem like an easy path, but it is also a dull and boring path and not attractive to anyone. Older people take more chances. They are daring... they conquer their shadows and fears with "no time to waste" energy. No one is ever too old to fulfill dreams and desires. Loading the senses up with delicious sights, sounds and tastes is a very good habit and a delightful way to keep your "child within" nurtured and joy filled. There are still adventures and stories to be shared and new ones to be discovered. At a certain age, conquering shadow sides is "not a big deal"...rather an exciting adventure. As they learn by example, maintaining a "Let's Do This" attitude is what keeps the younger generations around old folks. Choosing to have 70 "BE" the new 40 is a good plan. Remaining the oldest of the young and the youngest of the old is a balancing act that is well worth the effort.

In regard to keeping your list of *confidences* strong and continuing to serving you, being grateful and humble is so necessary. Being complacent, resting on your laurels or simply taking your good fortune of having virtues and talents for granted can make them literally fade away. Forget about reminiscing through scrap books when you can "live" a new scrap book! No matter what the treasure... appreciation and care is a given... although... sometimes we forget our blessings and start "counting sheep". No one has a list of *confidences* that can't be improved upon, maybe toned down a bit or highlighted. There isn't any room for the EGO on your *confidences* list. The sky is the limit when it comes to the "good stuff" of your make up...of what makes you: YOU.

.

CHAPTER 23

Try Something New

On the ride home from Tony Robbins fire walk, I felt as though I could conquer my mountains of complex, complicated tasks at hand... and I did! I had the power of Wonder Woman, the zeal of Joan of Arc and the compassion of Mother Teresa.   Just as vintage sterling silver needs buffing and shining, so too does your list of *confidences* need to be up updated and made ready for action. Mentally, physically and emotionally, a sense of freedom has to abound throughout your list of *confidences*. Tools need to be oiled, sharpened and used or they become rusty and useless. Emotional and real tools nearly have to stand at attention, ready to boost up any and all wishes, hopes and dreams on your shadow list. Pride will grow on your shadow side and in no time one or two shadows will be *"Welcomed to the Club of Confidences"*. My artist/writer friend is now a certified painter. This accomplishment and its success will pump up the know-how energy in her writing and acting skills. Soon, she will be a Jack of all Trades and she is loving it. She now has an official backup plan.

We are all so much the same and yet so different. Daily rituals are quite individual and private. We all begin and wind down our days in a myriad of unique, unto us alone... rituals that, in time, become hard wired and in a is way... don't demand much thought. Like the front and back covers of a book... we all wind up and unwind in special ways that work for us. In between the front and back covers, the pages of our books differ. As habits go, the start and finish of our days are so important and, happily, they don't take much thought. Early morning and late evening meditations...if only for a few minutes... don't take much thought, in fact an empty mind is the best way to begin meditating.

CHAPTER 24

Giving Is Receiving

Years ago the words: "For now and forever, for always and ever, little things mean a lot" is a line from a song that I remember hearing and loving on the radio, when I was a little girl. Little things: a kind gesture, a gentleman standing up when a woman enters the room, a stunning single rose...mean a lot and those gracious memories last forever. In so many small ways, there is so much that we can give to encourage others on their paths. Saying: "what a good boy" to a baby or a dog gets a huge smile and a wag of a tail. I'm in the habit of keeping some little "this-n-thats" in the car that I can give away... whenever and to whomever I choose. It's one of my forms of positive, uplifting communication. On the street, at the market, in class, in church... there isn't ever any discrimination as to "who gets what" and I never have a need to get anything back. I sort of "level the playing field" as I give little surprises all around town. A return of any kind diminishes the gift. Watching someone break into a huge smile ...that's the best gift I get back. Whatever your "feel good to others" activity is... no need to save your unique exchange. If you feel a giving spirit, no need to wait for special occasions or sunny days. Just because Jesus was born or for that matter...just because anyone was born, I don't feel that I have an obligation to run out and buy a present and wrap it and give it away. I give when I feel like it. Shadows disappear and *confidences* abound!

There is a guru who lives in a monastery here in California. Daily, his followers are inspired by him. A few years ago... the word got out that he was about to talk to his people for the last time. The following Sunday morning a horn, formed from mountain goat antler, was blown at sunrise. Everyone gathered... anxious to hear their guru's final words. His message was simple and profound: "my hope, my prayer is that everyone here and in the world, can learn to be kinder to one another". That was it. He hasn't spoken since that early Sunday morning on a hill at the monastery. Kindness is an arrow not a boomerang. It goes straight to the heart without a hand waiting for a return. Kindness is a full circle and complete virtue all unto itself.

"Sticks and stones will break my bones but names will never hurt me." Whoever put those untrue words together? They need to get back up on the horse and then ride on! Although not necessary, we all welcome sincere compliments. No one likes "name calling" or criticism. Having to put walls up to avoid negative energy or pretending that you are not bothered, simply does not work on my playground. The first moment I encounter a fake, phony person... I give them a mannerly smile and continue down the road. Toxic people don't have a place... well...anywhere. Like pesticides on plants, toxic people can kill the gentle spirits and good will of others.

CHAPTER 25

Accomplishments Have Rewards

Transferring confidences is a kind of virtual, magic figure eight shape. Just imagine moving your thoughts and actions from darkness into light, replacing negativity with positivity As we age, our hopes and desires change. We discover new *confidences* that in the past were shadows. Best part, you will use your *confidences* in your personal and business lives. "The proof is in the pudding". It is so satisfying when you accomplish something and have no need to "tell it to the world". The accomplishment comes with inner praise for a job well done. You won't have the slightest desire to "shout it from the highest hill or tell the golden daffodils". Growing up, when one of us kids "did a good job", we'd announce: "I get to take all the credit for this... you can't take any of the credit". This kind of energy grows as we grow. When we reach the point that the accomplishment has a built in satisfaction without reaching for outside accolades... then you have created a new *confidence*...put it on your list!

Your heart is a treasure chest...just for you. When something is done "in order to" get praise...the depth of personal "I DID IT" satisfaction is limited. Remember running up the down escalator when you were a mischievous kid?

We'd all run up, as the escalator was going down. We'd take a few seconds to catch our breath and then... continue running up the down escalator. Finally we'd reach the top and jump for joy off the last moving stair. NOW: you can let the world know how great you were and feel your successful energy dwindle away, or you can infuse your inner "feel good" praise, teach your pals how you did it and move on to the next challenge at hand. Again, knowing when and where to take a rest, is a healthy *confidence*.   As adults, waiting around for applause and pats on the back are not *confidence* builders. Your inner compass is always there for you. Self gratification is a complete feeling. Day by day, action by action... where there isn't a reward or a need for praise for a job well done is a major *confidence*. A few words on paper on my front door: "Today, do something for someone who will never find out it came from you".   Great masters in any field don't have a desire for ballyhoos or applause. Accolades can diminish the creation. It doesn't matter if a project is large or small, when earned... people will joyfully give kudos to inventors, artists, managers and team leaders. There are always more projects on the table. Success has a built in *confidence* that spurs you on to the next goal. Standing around waiting for praise, is such a waste of time and dissipates a feeling of goodness and self-satisfaction.

Every so often a project, friendship or job becomes stagnant and stops moving ahead. Even though you are on "a road to nowhere" your shadow side says: "just keep moving on with it". This is when it's a good plan to *"Transfer Your Confidence"* of courage, foresight and leadership of "self to self" and get off that train. No matter what the situation, it takes guts to call it quits. When it is totally clear that positive energy isn't any part of this situation, it takes honesty and your truth to step away. You might feel a loss, but the gain of personal dignity and a fresh open space is greater than any loss imaginable. When you keep your *confidences* "at the ready" that energy can step in like a soldier and get you out of harm's way and into the fresh open space that belongs to you... a fresh open space where you can begin to move forward once again. Shadows begin to disappear when replaced with *confidences*. Reversed, we can add to our *confidences*. "I've never tried that and oh my gosh, I'm really good at it!" Keep doing "that", until it becomes natural and becomes a *confidence* to try something new again and to share your success in a helpful way to others. *Confidences* are not EGO based rather grateful and humble places of the heart. When we are the leader at the game of: "follow the leader", our paths and our ideas must be inviting and we must be inviting as well. We are magnets. Take a look at how and what you are attracting. If the path is unattractive, try to change course quickly.

CHAPTER 26

Love

Here is the most basic way to strengthen any and all *confidences*: LOVE. Starting with SELF love (some call it "the God within") and then: "self-care-love". Perhaps you could upgrade your body lotion and use it twice every day. Treat yourself every month to a massage, facial and a mani-pedi. How about. in-joying a long delicious (for the body & soul) lunch...often...with a dear friend. Here is another plan of SELF fulfillment action: choose a virtue. "BE" and share that virtue for an entire day... at work, in the gym, throughout correspondences like emails and office messages. Allow your daily virtues to infuse your life at home, on the phone or simply on the street. Virtues like gratefulness, kindness and generosity while giving compliments and smiles throughout your day. At the close of a "virtue" kind of day, you might think: "OK that's over". The next day, either choose another virtue or choose it the night before and "sleep on it". Wake up in your virtue or forget about this "virtue idea" and go about your day. Believe me; it's so easy to make a difference when your day is infused with a virtue. It will energize you and build up a *confidence* or two and perhaps ... create a new *confidence* as shadows disappear.

"There is no need to fear, underdog is here" Wally Cox. Growing up, I was "the black sheep of our family". Funny, I was the only one with dark hair. Back in the day, when our parents were interrogating all of us over "spilled milk" and such... I'd simply say: "I did IT. Oh by the way, what was IT?" When I was a little "tom boy", I didn't have any *confidences* to transfer. Thank God for my art and my sense of humor. Daily, they saved me. I was Murphy's Law personified: "anything that can go wrong will go wrong". I know today, that I can thank my bottom position on the family totem pole for my adult life quest for happiness, knowledge and love. I have searched, studied and found that I am pretty OK. As Richard Bach wrote: "We teach best what we most need to learn." Slowly but surely, with a bit of backpedaling, I'm learning that "the past is the past" the NOW is great and the future is bright. Even today, when someone is upset or grumpy or not responsive, I think to myself: "either you caused or you can fix it". Day by day, less and less... I am letting go of that philosophy and more and more I am choosing positive thoughts and actions. *Transferring my Confidence* to: a very strong and positive belief in me... over the bad little girl... that still resides inside of me is nothing short of the most important game in my life.

If I don't keep control of the noise in my mind and change it to music, it could render me useless.

Eckhart Tolle is a renowned thinker whom I have long respected. As an unhappy child raised in Germany, he too was in a search for the truth…for what was right and good and joyful. It's nearly synchronic (a concept studied at length by another great German thinker: Carl Jung) how much our childhoods and early adulthoods were both driven by a search for the truth. Once Eckhart became perfectly clear that it was his internal thinking and awareness that would bring him joy, he found bliss. He realized: rather than searching through unending sources of outside forces that influenced him in the past, he found it was an inside, rewarding and everlasting job. He said: "the primary cause of unhappiness is never the situation, but your thoughts about it. The power for creating a better future is contained in the present moment. You create a good future by creating a good present. In the stillness of your presence, you can feel your own formless and timeless reality as the unmanifested life that animates your physical form. You can then feel the same life deep within EVERY OTHER HUMAN and EVERY OTHER CREATURE. You look beyond the veil of form and separation. This is the realization of ONENESS. THIS IS LOVE."

Years ago, coinciding with his thoughts, I wrote: TO WIN/GO: WITHIN... whenever I'm stopped, confused or frustrated, it's my mantra.   Eckhart taught me that no matter how bad it gets: I can accept it, change it or "ease on down the 'Wizard of Oz' road" away from it all. Hanging out with your inner self is by no means a "cop out" or a waste of time; rather it is empowering. Outside influences bombard us constantly. We don't need to run and hide, we just need to live in the NOW, NOW,NOW moments one after another after another, accepting the truth and moving away from negativity while gaining a fresh and resilient spirit. Bay Area people live in earthquake zones. We can all take a note from the earthquake zone. The world is constantly shifting. For sure, life is a balancing act. As long as we are flexible, as long as we "go with the flow" there will be less conflicts and more harmony. Sorry to break the news, but the external world is not here to satisfy us. We can all live a "take it or leave it" life. Aliveness, clarity and intelligence will abound when we choose a joy filled, honest path.

David Crosby, of the Crosby, Stills Nash and Young rock band, was born into privilege. His early adult life was palpable with acrimony spread through every business and personal relationship. Today, he is healthy, clean and grateful. Although the words to his songs are wonderful...the timely "sound bite" that hit me like a ton of heavenly bricks the other day (in an Alec Baldwin "Here's The Thing" Interview) and resonates with my belief was: "more than anything else, creativity lifts you up. The creator and those who enjoy the work will truly be lifted up."

CHAPTER 27

Trust Yourself

Trust your *confidences*, honor your *confidences*, and check in with yourself ...often . "If you don't use it; you'll lose it". DO what you DO.... often. You might be a pro today; tomorrow could be a different story. Pick up those knitting needles, that paint brush, that spatula and...for no apparent reason... make something for someone you love. The process is as enjoyable as the product. Seeing a smile of delight and surprise on an unsuspecting customer ...is priceless. Strengthening your *confidences*...by using them...will weaken your shadows. A Buddhist priest once told me: "you don't have to spend time with your enemies.   Still in silence...you can love them. Have them in the door to your heart, give them tea and then send them out the back door". He reminded me of my yoga teacher: "go into a pose with grace and dignity and then go out of the pose the same way". Daily, I use this "virtual talisman" as a gracious way to live my life. "We're all in this together"...don't be afraid to reach out for help or to give help.

Hedy Lamarr was proud to say: "I felt that I had served my time as a purppet; analysis gave me great freedom of emotions and fantastic Confidence". She was forever touted as being one of the most beautiful women in the world. "Any girl can be glamorous; all you have to do is stand there and look stupid". That was far from the kind of life she lead. Although she invented: "Frequency Hopping Spread Spectrum" FHSS which we all use today with our cell phones, in our cars and on TV, she was still treated like a "glam girl" rather than for her genius. She defied "pretty girl" customs saying: "I'm a sworn enemy of convention. I despise the conventional in anything, even the arts." And my favorite Hedy Lamarr quote: "Hope and curiosity about the future seemed better than guarantees. The unknown was always so attractive to me... and still is!"

When Eckhart Tolle preached: "birds and flowers are here on this planet for pure pleasure, beauty, enjoyment and awe", he reminded me that I need to "stop and smell the roses" more often. Maybe we could schedule 5 to 15 minutes out of every hour just to breathe in nature and all of "her" gifts. We miss so much and become so small when we rush through every day. Fifty plus years ago, here is another "right on time" Hedy Lamarr quote: "The world isn't getting any easier. With all of these new inventions I believe that people are hurried more and pushed more. The hurried way is not the right way; you need time for everything-time: time to work, time to play, time to rest".

HABITS... this is a subject that could be covered quickly in a paragraph or in depth in an entire book. Let's try a kind of "Cliff Notes" overview. First of all...there are good and "not so good" habits. We can always improve on a good habit and... with the help of a *confidence* or two, we can adjust or let go of a "not so good" habit. A guy who stops by a bar for an "on the way home cocktail" EVERY night...has a habit that has a little bit of control of his life. It isn't a daily choice, rather a daily habit. On the other hand, there is another guy, who stops by the gym on the way to work and has chosen a habit that will empower his day. We all have many rituals that empower us. For example: journaling and meditation are both considered good habits. I have a friend who meditates while showering EVERY morning. What a great way to start the morning! He says the water even feels better. He cleans his mind and body! A ritual of having dessert every evening without even thinking about it: "not so good" a habit.   We don't have to put the brakes on full throttle to stop a bad habit. We can just cut back slowly, then stop and replace a bad ingrained habit with a better, more happy and healthy habit. Going "cold turkey" can be quite jarring and can actually set us back a few paces.

25+ years ago, the band "Chicago" had a hit song: "I'm addicted to you babe, yer a bad habit to break". There are a handful of terrific and successful "Anonymous" meetings for people with "hard habits to break". While they are all well and good and anonymous meetings, we all have *confidences* that we can draw on to help us out of bad habits. Every day is a new day. Remember, you can break a habit in 21 days. Through the inner strength of our *confidences*, we can break habits that tend to control our lives rather than enhance our lives. Many baby steps are great. We can slow down a "not so good habit". Now and then, we can choose to treat ourselves. It's just that when we choose "now & then" and "then & now" then the time can slip into a bad habit and land on our shadow list. One day at a time. Put stars on your calendar. Count your days that are filled with pride. Be your own coach. Be an example to kids. Empowered or devoured… it's your choice.

It's never a good practice to end a day in an unsettled misunderstanding or argument. Just "sleep on it" doesn't give you a good night's sleep.   Even if you are in the right and you know it... maybe be the bigger person and let the other guy have the last word. Your peace, your joy will become richer and you will sleep like a baby. *Confidences* can become weak and fade away or they can become stronger and more alive. Nothing stays the same. Everything changes. Might as well "not sweat the small stuff" because the situation can, for no particular reason, become a huge EGO based event. You can "stick to your guns", be true to yourself and just "let it go".

For years, I have had this pal who thought he was his car. Then he thought he was his terrific job. For a while, he even thought he was his hair! As he matured (thank GOD) he realized that it's about "what's inside" that really matters...not exterior affectations. Once he GOT IT... that "it's an inside job", everyone loved being around him. No more games, no more "phony baloney BS", no more putting his "stuff" on a pedestal. He simply became REAL and began to live in his truth. For me, this kind of homework...this kind of evolving...took years of therapy, classes, mentors and I'm still trying to "BE" that person in the mirror. I studied A Course in Miracles, Science of Mind, Sterling Institute of Relationship, Tony Robins' seminars, Werner Erhard's classes, Buddhism, Catholicism, Unity

Thought, The Four Agreements, various "self-help" books and tapes, workshops and retreats just to find myself and to be happy. I'm still involved in many on line classes. I'll never have life figured out...but the process is comforting and fulfilling.

.

CHAPTER 28
Everything Becomes Better

Once I thought of: *"Transferring my Confidences"...* all of the puzzle pieces came into a shape forming a beautiful picture...and a beautiful life. Today, when I'm down, I don't stay there very long. I just take a look at my list of *confidences,* get into a grateful state of mind and do something nice for myself or for others. It is an immediate paradigm shift and like mom kissing you... "Everything becomes better".

"When your luck is batting zero, you've gotta have heart,
Don't sit around and mope you've gotta have hope"

Today was just that kind of day expressed in these words. I was batting zero. I tried my logical, happy go lucky" *confidence...* it didn't kick in. Then I thought about a lovely friend who had just lost her husband. I got up off the pity pot and began making a collection of jewelry for her. Matching one of my many Italian scarves, I made a necklace, bracelet, earrings and a tender ring to replace her wedding ring. I was lost up in her and in this empowering process. As I headed down to the post office, I realized that I had just used my creative *confidence* to put a healing smile on my friend's face and heart. As a bonus to this process, I was on top of the world! Yup, when your luck is batting zero…yah gotta have miles and miles of heart. If the proof is in the pudding, then *Transferring my Confidence* really worked that afternoon! Just thinking about that day, energizes me right now!

These days, "BF" means Best Friend. How cool it could be to call your God (whatever that may mean to you)…your "BF". A few days ago, I just decided to try this idea on for size. It fits like a glove. I'm finding myself talking to God in colloquial, non-formal and sometimes even in slang terms. I am not, by any means, showing any amount of disrespect. On the contrary, I am being pals with my God. "Come on God, fix this…I've tried my best but I'm stuck…so PLEASE fix it… after all you are God!" Or: "I'm jammed…in a huge hurry…help me get organized and get outta here before I get fired". There are many hymns and lyrics that talk about having a friend in The Lord, God, and Jesus and in Allah. St. Teresa of Avila was known for her "talks with God". She didn't pull any punches. She took command of her needs and asked for direction and guidance. She asked God to answer her concerns, to be of comfort and to heal the sick.

Indeed God was her "BF". In no time at all, we can all find soothing solace in our God. Don't forget these 4 simple words: "TO WIN/GO WITHIN". Soon our relationship with our "higher authority" can become one of our *confidences*. It isn't necessary to go to church or read a book...it's an inside job...SELF 2 SELF. It has already become second nature for me to talk to God. As long as these conversations have naturally looped into my life, I am finding a rich *confidence* and security in my new "BF" relationship. There are many songs about talking to the trees, to the birds and now an ongoing conversation with God. That, to me...is very cool!

How often do you receive a "for no reason" sweet card in the mail? I'm not talking about an email. I'm talking about a REAL note, a letter in the US Mail with a "forever fun" stamp on it. Also, with a hand written address and from address on the envelope. Not too often...right? Although it is so exciting, so touching to see a REAL hand addressed letter that arrives nearly lost in junk mail and bills....who has the time today to actually write a "for no reason" letter? "Kindness" is said to be one of the most treasured of virtues ... a virtue that deserves to be protected, shared and nurtured. A kind letter might seem like a waste of time, but writing it and sending it off will empower your positive energy and build a new *confidence* of more depth of care and more sensitivity of character. I just dreamed up a quick way to write a "for no reason" letter. #1: Compliment the person. "I was thinking about you today and I just wanted you to know... how much you mean to me"... or "I want you to know what a positive force you have been in my life"... or "how often I think about you and how much I treasure our friendship"...or, or, or. #2: "everything is good with me" #3: Wishing you continued happiness" That's IT! So now, I'm going to try this process and actually time it...starting right now! OK... that took all of 4 & 1/2 minutes!   As James Brown sang: "I feel good, just like I knew that I would now. Yup, I feel good...so good I've got YOU, YOU & YOU!"   Maybe you might give this "for no reason" letter a try and just imagine your friend reading it. The process takes less than five minutes and will give someone a day of heartfelt sunshine. After writing a few "for no reason" letters, the *confidence* gained is an empowerment of a generous and kind interaction. Believe me, at some future date, you will need your friend. Your note will make your connection fresh, real and honest...honestly! The following words are from a sweet and yet sad Frank Sinatra   song: " I'm gonna sit right down and write myself a letter, and make believe it came from you'.

CHAPTER 29

Appreciation

I hadn't ever thought of appreciation as a *confidence*. This morning, after chewing on appreciation as a *confidence*, along with my toast and eggs, I gave "appreciation" a slice spot on my pie chart. We carried on a pleasant conversation about how blessed we are to have such a lovely breakfast, in a beautiful room while listening to soft music twirling... like ribbons in the sunshine... throughout our house. My husband commented: "I don't ever want to get used to the ordinary events of life. To me they are "extra ordinary". Just mentioning our blessed breakfast time, gave me pause to realize and remember the richness in the daily gifts of life that I tend to take for granted. In my office, I have a movie screen sized horizontal shade, just behind this computer, that moves up and down. Each morning, as I lift the shade and greet the day, I feel like I am opening the curtains to a magical Broadway play. We live on a canal, surrounded by Mother Nature's wonder. Every day, in a grateful way, Eckhart Tolle's words: "Birds and flowers were created simply for our pure, exquisite pleasure" come to mind. Every morning, no matter what the weather might be, I experience nature at its very best as I pull the shades up and embrace the day...it nearly envelopes me in a cloud of deep amazement and wonder. In gratitude, I stop and breathe it all in. So why then is appreciation a *confidence*? Perhaps every "appreciation" strengthens my will to be strong rather than weak, to soldier on, to be content and grateful... moment to moment.

In the book: "Gulliver's Travels"... the hero's boat sinks and he is swept ashore. Exhausted, he falls fast asleep on the beach. While sleeping, tiny little six inch tall Lilliputians capture Gulliver by tying him down with bits of thread. He tries to break away, but finally he gives up and is kind and grateful to the little guys. They fed him, released him and all ended happily ever after. In the opposite way (and this is a stretch of the imagination) every day, common-to-all "appreciations" that occur on our paths of life, when recognized and assimilated into our lives, will diffuse our shadows and make them disappear. Imagine, after a day punctuated with "appreciations", your car is rear ended. Trust me (because it happened to me recently) I just rolled with the punches rather than punching the other driver out! Acknowledged "appreciations," in and around you each day, do soften any blow. Look around, you will see... as you sense...oh so much to "appreciate". Next, carry on with more joy in your heart. Belief in this process we call life, indeed, "appreciation" is my new "*confidence*".

When turning my bedroom light switch on this morning, I paused and thought: "when I switch this lamp off at the end of the day...the room becomes dark... but the electricity is still there". In the same way, there is oh so much that can be accessed within my mind that may never have ever been "switched on". What an amazing discovery...that an abundance of creativity and knowledge is here for me "at the ready" any time of day or night! This is such a prime example of: "*Transferring a Confidence*". Positive energy, like electricity, can be accessed as easily as flipping a switch and thus... turning on a quality that I have long sought after is available 24/7!

CONCLUSION

Intimacy, taken apart, means INTO-ME-YOU-SEE. As we build up our *confidences* and choose to create new ones, we become more open to sharing our gifts, our blessings and our love. Like animals that shoot out needles, unattractive scents and even change their colors... we too camouflage our true selves until we begin to take pride in who we are. Personal homework, accepting our gifts, becoming grateful for our virtues and sharing joy is all a part of being human. There is a lot going on deep down in the soil before even a speck of a green plant appears to greet the sun. We too have deep soul searching and growing up to do before we can feel free to express ourselves to the world. "Just because" is enough of a reason to share your inner self whenever an opportunity comes along. Your *confidences* will forever be the bedrock of your personality and the way you choose to live your life. Refine them, use them and, by example, encourage others to get a list of their confidences going as well. Without confidence, we tend to spend too much time patching emotions up, sliding backwards and engaging in hopeless wishing. Let's not ever forget, we all have what we need to live an extra ordinary life. Red, yellow and blue are the three basic colors. An almost infinite number of colors can be mixed by using these three colors. Let's take red as your body, yellow as your spirit and blue as your mind. There is no time like the present to work with these three parts of being human...and together with our own unique individual *confidences*...let's all create and share a rainbow kind of life.

ABOUT THE AUTHOR

"If you are a hammer, everything is a nail". Kathleen has been "making stuff" ever since she could hold a crayon in her baby hand. From the canvas to the kitchen… she can't go very many hours without making something from scratch… without a recipe or an idea in mind. Like jumping from rock to rock across a creek, Kathleen has always had mentors, guides, teachers and people who have believed in her unique process of creating art.

Years after graduating from Dominican University, she made jewelry for her showcase at Saks Fifth Avenue. She writes for several magazines and publishes a blog: (fashionwithflair.blogspot.com). After joining Screen Actors Guild, she took on an acting career. She wrote commercials for Ketchum International, does motivational speaking and is involved in many Bay Area Charities. The Nob Hill Gazette gave her the honor of being "one of the four most fashionable women in The Bay Area". Kathleen loves "the hunt". From resale shops to flea markets around the globe, she finds treasures, repurposes them and makes them her own. Like Hansel and Gretel, Kathleen leaves trails of laughter and love on her path. She has a few favorite lines: "Do you know where the lamplighter is?" "No, but I know where he's been". "Master, isn't this the most beautiful sunset you've ever seen?" "Yes, until you mentioned it". Her favorite seven words: "once upon a time…. happily ever after". She hopes that this book will help to fill in the middle of those seven words.

Made in the USA
San Bernardino, CA
10 February 2019